LARRY GELBART has writ[...]
stage. For television he wrote

Hour, *The Danny Kaye Show*
known for developing and co-
television series *M*A*S*H*. H[...] [...]*The
Notorious Landlady* (1960), *The Wrong Box* (1966, co-authored
with Burt Shevelove), *Oh, God!* (1977), *Movie, Movie* (1981) and
Tootsie (1982). For the stage he also wrote the books for the
musicals *The Conquering Hero* (1961) and *City of Angels* (1989)
and his plays include *Jump* (1971), *Sly Fox* (1976, based on
Jonson's *Volpone*) and *Mastergate* (1989). Amongst many other
awards, he received a Tony for both *A Funny Thing Happened on
the Way to the Forum* and *City of Angels*.

BURT SHEVELOVE made his Broadway debut as the director
and co-author of the revue *Small Wonder* (1948). He directed the
award-winning productions of *Hallelujah, Baby!* (1968) and *No,
No, Nanette* (1971), for which he also restructured the book of the
original 1925 production, adapted and directed Wlilliam Gillette's
play *Too Much Johnson* (1964), wrote the book for and directed the
musical *The Frogs* (1974, adapted from the comedy of Aristophanes,
with music and lyrics by Stephen Sondheim) and wrote and
directed the musical *Happy New Year* (1980, adapted from Philip
Barry's play *Holiday*). For the screen he co-authored with Larry
Gelbart and co-produced *The Wrong Box* (1966), and for television
he produced, directed and wrote hundreds of shows starring,
amongst others, Jack Benny, Art Carney, Judy Garland, Frank
Sinatra and Barbra Streisand. At the time of his death in 1982, Mr
Shevelove was preparing a musical version of *The Front Page*.

STEPHEN SONDHEIM is one of the most influential and
innovative artists working in contemporary musical theatre. He
wrote the lyrics for *West Side Story* (1957), *Gypsy* (1959) and *Do I
Hear a Waltz?* (1965) and the complete scores for *Anyone Can
Whistle* (1964), *Company* (1970), *Follies* (1971), *A Little Night
Music* (1973), *The Frogs* (1974), *Pacific Overtures* (1976),
Sweeney Todd (1979), *Merrily We Roll Along* (1981), *Sunday in
the Park with George* (1984), *Into the Woods* (1987), *Assassins*
(1990), *Passion* (1994) and *Bounce* (2003). *Side By Side By
Sondheim* (1976), *Marry Me A Little* (1980) and *Putting It
Together* (1992) are anthologies of his works as composer and
lyricist. He also composed the film scores for *Stavisky* and *Reds*
and songs for the film *Dick Tracy*. In 1983 he was elected to the
American Academy and Institute of Arts and Letters, and in 1990
he was the first Cameron Mackintosh Visiting Professor of
Contemporary Theatre at Oxford University.

Also by Stephen Sondheim

With George Furth:
COMPANY
GETTING AWAY WITH MURDER

With James Goldman:
FOLLIES

With James Lapine:
INTO THE WOODS
PASSION
SUNDAY IN THE PARK WITH GEORGE

With Arthur Laurents and Jule Styne:
GYPSY

With John Weidman:
ASSASSINS
PACIFIC OVERTURES

With Hugh Wheeler:
A LITTLE NIGHT MUSIC
SWEENEY TODD

A FUNNY THING HAPPENED ON THE WAY TO THE FORUM

Book by
BURT SHEVELOVE
and
LARRY GELBART

Music and Lyrics by
STEPHEN SONDHEIM

Based on the plays of
PLAUTUS

Introduced by Larry Gelbart

NICK HERN BOOKS
London
www.nickhernbooks.co.uk

A Nick Hern Book

A Funny Thing Happened on the Way to the Forum
first published in Great Britain as a paperback original in 2004
by Nick Hern Books Limited, 14 Larden Road, London W3 7ST

Cover Image: detail from design by Nappi. Reproduced with permission.

Typeset by Country Setting, Kingsdown, Kent CT14 8ES
Printed and bound in Great Britain by Bookmarque, Croydon

A CIP catalogue record for this book is available from
the British Library

ISBN 1 85459 145 2

TO AND FROM
T.M.P.

Contents

Introduction

by Larry Gelbart

As a rule, authors suspect the quality of any work that is written quickly and rather painlessly. *A Funny Thing Happened on the Way to the Forum* was never an object of that sort of suspicion. The only aspect of the project that ever came fast and free of any pain was the dialogue. Even when we lost our way in terms of plotting, and I cannot tell you how many man-hours (women- and children-hours, as well) we spent in a wilderness of our own creation, we were never at a loss for words, funny words, mostly-funny words, or words that led up to the funny words, or funny words that paved the way for even funnier words. (Lovers of modesty will find little to their liking in this foreword, since I have absolutely none to offer when it comes to *Forum.* Nearly thirty years after its first performance, and having, in the intervening period, written enough words to circle the globe and the Old Globe dozens of times, it remains for me the best piece of work I've been lucky enough to see my name on.)

Irwin Shaw once advised all writers, in order to withstand criticism from without and compromise from within, to be vain about their work. Until *A Funny Thing Happened on the Way to the Forum,* I confess there was little I had done that warranted any sort of vanity.

The initial idea to do the show was the late Burt Shevelove's. Burt had done an embryonic version of a Roman comedy in his university days and had long felt that a professional, full-blown Broadway production would have every chance of success.

Although Burt and I had worked together on many television shows during the 1950s, we had never functioned before as a writing team. Burt produced and directed several comedy/variety shows that I had written in that period; working in separate capacities, we learned that we laughed at the same things and, happily, always at the same time.

Our goal was to construct a musical comedy based on the style and spirit of the twenty-six surviving plays of Titus Maccius Plautus, the third-century Roman playwright, who invented all the devices of theatrical comedy, teaching amphitheatre audiences up and down Caesar's Circuit to laugh for the first time at character and situation instead of that old staple they found so amusing, bloodshed.

Certainly, there was comedy in everyday life before Plautus set quill to parchment, but it was he who created comic conventions and made use of humorous wordplay within the discipline of well-made plays.

With Stephen Sondheim as the third member of the team (it was to be the first Broadway show for which he created words and music; before *Forum* Steve had *merely* supplied the lyrics for *West Side Story* and *Gypsy),* we began the task of reading and dissecting the writings of and about Plautus, extracting from his works a character here, a relationship there, and then went about creating a considerable amount of new material, both dramatic and musical, as connective tissue to bond our work to his.

What a treat he was to research! How incredibly Plautus's aged, ageless writings based on man's gift for silliness, for pomposity and hypocrisy, have survived; how well it all stood up, the comedy that would serve as fodder not only for the theatre, but for future stand-up comedians as well. Digging about as archaeologists might have, what unbelievable treasure we found in his plays, a catacomb filled with nothing but funnybones. It was as though Titus (I feel he would forgive the name-dropping) had written some great and generous last will and testament, a comic estate, and that Burt, Steve, and I had been appointed his heirs.

There they were, in the pages of Plautus, appearing for our pleasure for the first time anywhere: the brash Prologus, working very much in the manner of a modern-day master of ceremonies, addressing his remarks directly to the audience, hitting them with one-liners, warning them to sit up and pay attention and not to go to sleep during the play that was to follow. There were the sly servants, those wily slaves, scheming and plotting and outwitting everyone in sight, constantly getting the upper hand on the upper class, which was largely composed of senile skirt-chasers and henpecked husbands, very often one and the same; domineering matrons, Gorgon-like women, past their prime in every aspect of life but possessiveness; lovesick young men, so much in love they were sickening; and, of course, comely courtesans with hair and hearts of gold that you couldn't bring home without fear of possibly offending your mother – and the certainty of arousing your father; page after page of disguise and mistaken identity, scene after scene of double takes and double meanings.

We were, of course, not Plautus's only benefactors. From the sublime Shakespeare to the somewhat less-so sitcoms, those writers who, through the ages, have presented audiences with surrogate fools acting out their own foibles (each member of the crowd, secure in the belief that he or she is above ridicule, that it is the person in the *next* seat who is being so portrayed), we are all indebted to Titus Maccius Plautus, high priest of low comedy, inventor of the genre, builder of the machine on which all theatre humour has run for over two millennia.

I believe it is safe to say that there is not a joke form, comic character, or farcical situation that exists today that does not find its origin in Plautus's work. *Forum* contains at least one taste of his original flavour. When Miles Gloriosus, the impossibly pompous, braggart warrior, gets a huge laugh (and he always does) by stating 'I am a parade!' the audience is responding to a line that is over two thousand years old.

Our goal was not to modernise the master. That is an ongoing process we preferred to leave to others. What we hoped to prove was that Plautus's characters (always one-dimensional) and his style of plotting (which could be as complicated as a Rubik's cube) were timeless. If the three of us occasionally resembled croquet wickets during our labours, it's because we spent so much time bending over backward to avoid using anachronisms (one such line which we rejected, and which we related to the writers of the *Forum* screenplay, found its way into a scene in the movie in which Pseudolus, the leading character, wanting to know about the quality of the wine he's being served, asks, 'Was 1 a good year?').

We were after more than purity, however. We were not simply out to prove some esoteric point that would have had an appreciative audience of three. We wanted a commercial as well as an artistic success. We were confident we could have both. Cocky would be more accurate. More than simply confidence is required to get a musical comedy on the boards. Vanity all on its own is not that much help either.

We knew that we were grounding our show in an element that had been long missing from the theatre scene. Over the years, Broadway, in its development of the musical comedy, had improved the quality of the former at the expense of a good deal of the latter. Musicals had come to be populated by performers who could sell a melody and a set of lyrics but who couldn't deliver a punchline in a handbasket. It was a talent they had no need for, since punchlines had all but disappeared. The Rodgerses and Harts and Hammersteins, the Lerners and Loewes, brilliant men of music and artists of great refinement, had created a vulgarity vacuum, a space we were happy, even anxious to fill.

Our Roman comedy opened in New York on May 8, 1962, complete with leggy showgirls being chased from house to house by cunning slaves, who, in drag a few scenes later, found *themselves* being chased by their own lecherous masters, unsuspecting dupes high on love potions prepared by these very same slaves, using recipes that called for such exotic ingredients as mare's sweat.

The show that *Time* magazine called 'good clean, dirty fun' has been running somewhere everywhere in the world for the last twenty-seven years. There was a time when the three of us thought it was going to take at least that long to finish writing it.

Steve has said that 'the book of *Forum* plays like such a romp it seems it might have been dashed off in a weekend, and yet it took four years to write.' I disagree with him only slightly. While it does, or at least should, play like a romp, I remember it taking us closer to five years to dash it off. That's approximately two hundred and sixty weekends – and most of the weekdays in between – which was all well and good for Plautus, who was that most helpful of collaborators, a dead one (even more helpful, so were his agents and lawyers), but for those of us among the living it was a big chunk of time.

A Roman Comedy was its working title. We were far too busy trying to get the piece right to take any time out to think about what some lucky marquee would one day read if we ever actually completed a final draft. There were to be ten drafts in all before we arrived at the last, merciful version of the book and score that represented the most successful execution of our vision. It's not that we kept getting it wrong all the time. It was more a matter of never getting it right all at the same time.

In the process, we rewrote and rewrote endlessly. Rewrote it, rethought it, restructured it. You name it, we redid it. It seemed a lifetime before we permitted ourselves to write that sweetest of all words in the vocabulary of the theatre: 'Curtain.'

Only then did we dare christen it, if one can use that verb in connection with a pagan comedy. Why the particular title we hit on? Since we wanted to suggest that the play was a comedy without actually using that word, we picked the phrase 'A funny thing happened on the way to' because that's the beginning of a stock opening line which comics have used for ages. 'Forum' was chosen to complete the title because we wanted the audience to think immediately of Rome.

But it took us hundreds and hundreds of pages before our comedy was ready for its naming day. And probably just as many measures of music, and reams of rhymes. Steve has said that he threw more songs out of the score for *Forum* than he's ever had to on any other show he's done since. Whole numbers – not fragments or starts with no finishes – written, polished, perfected, and then cut from the show.

For those of you who keep score of scores:

'I Do Like You.' A duet between Pseudolus and Hysterium, in which the first slave shamelessly butters up the second, who is reluctant to join in on some servant/master scam. Cut.

'There's Something About a War.' A hymn to mayhem and massacre, sung by the vainglorious Miles Gloriosus. Cut.

'Echo Song.' A solo for a courtesan from the house of Lycus named Philia. A virgin, she sings the song to the boy next door, Hero, her co-virgin. Replaced by 'That'll Show Him,' but restored in a revival.

'Love Is in the Air.' Originally, the show's opening song, performed as a soft-shoe dance and sung by Prologus, who was played by the same actor who portrayed Senex. When 'Comedy Tonight' replaced this number, Pseudolus became the Prologus and the only trace of 'Love Is in the Air' that remains in the show is as instrumental background to the opening of Act Two. Much has been written about what a lifesaver 'Comedy Tonight' proved to be in getting the show off the ground in the proper manner and style. It also provided us with a happy landing when, reprised at the final curtain, it served as a witty, musical wrap-up, one that had eluded us from the show's inception.

'Invocation.' The first of three tries at an opening number.

'The House of Marcus Lycus.' Reduced to one verse during the New Haven tryout.

'Your Eyes Are Blue.' Cut in New Haven.

'The Gaggle of Geese.' Written for Erronius. Cut before rehearsals began.

'Farewell.' Added for the Los Angeles revival in 1971.

'What Do You Do with a Woman?' A song for the innocent Hero in which he asks for advice on the subject of amour from his far more experienced friend and next-door neighbour, Vino.

Vino? Those of you who know the play know there is no one named Vino in it. Those of you unfamiliar with it can read the pages which follow for as many years as we took to write them and not find anyone anywhere named Vino, not even a mention of him, for Vino was to suffer the fate that befalls many a dramatic character who does not survive the embryonic stage – he died in playbirth. Having survived through two or three drafts, Vino developed a severe case of anaemia of purpose and never made it to the fourth.

We planned the action of *Forum* to take place before the entrances to three houses on a street in ancient Rome. In the centre, the house of Senex, a patrician, and his family. To one side of Senex, the house of Marcus Lycus, a dealer of courtesans, a trader of tarts; on the other, the house of another patrician, Erronius, who has been abroad for some time.

From day one, that original geography remained intact. Early on, however, we had installed Vino in the house of Erronius, as the son the old man leaves behind to be looked after by his household slave, Hysterium. Vino was a dissolute youth, much given to wine, women, and, hopefully, a song that wouldn't be cut. His constant companions were twin courtesans, purchased from Lycus, who were forever entwining themselves around various of Vino's limbs, a pair of torrid tourniquets.

All of this kept Hysterium in a perpetual state of hysteria. He lived in fear of the flogging or worse he'd receive when

Erronius returned for allowing his son to pursue such a decadent and expensive life.

Vino's best friend was Hero, the son of Senex, whose own slave was Pseudolus, a name we borrowed from the title of a play by Plautus. The idea of twins comes from yet another, entitled *The Menachmae*. It was Pseudolus in whom Hysterium confided, looked to for advice on how to deal with the excesses of his young charge.

Pseudolus, too, had his hands full with *his* master, Hero, the only son of Senex and his wife of too many years, Domina. (Plautus was, naturally, the inventor of jokes on marital strife. In one of his works, two Roman citizens meet on the street. The first citizen asks the second, 'How's your wife?' The second citizen replies with a sigh, 'Immortal.')

Hero, too, is smitten with a young woman from the wrong side of the stage, having fallen in love with the most recent addition to Lycus's inventory, the adorable, totally vapid Philia (about whom one might have asked, 'Was 1 a good IQ?') Pseudolus's task was to keep Hero's parents from finding out that their son coveted a common courtesan.

You will, of course, have immediately spotted the duplication of situations in the houses of Senex and Erronius, the common problem shared by Pseudolus and Hysterium. Not being as bright as you, it took us a couple of years to become aware of these redundancies. Once we did, we decided that Vino had to go. It was quite painless: over a number of pages we got the character drunk and then arranged for him to have a head-on collision with an eraser. He never saw it coming. We then moved Hysterium into the house of Senex, giving him the position of head slave, which created one more obstacle for Pseudolus to contend with in handling his problems with Hero. Best of all, the changes served to make the centre house the centre of the audience's attention.

These revisions and others like them necessitated countless further alterations. If one could take *Forum* apart, unscrew the back of it, so to speak, it would be not unlike looking at the works of a computer or the jumble of different-coloured wires telephone repairmen deal in. The play is that dense, that tangled. Add or subtract one character and his or her absence or altered presence affects the behaviour of every other character in the piece.

'Simplify it,' George Abbott told the authors. 'Stop writing all that "wrong-note" music,' Leonard Bernstein told the composer. But we had no choice other than to write the show our way, which required the exhausting exercise of finding out what that way was.

In preparing this foreword, I'm indebted to Steve Sondheim for helping me recall a number of details I'd long forgotten. Thank God for his memory. My own, its warranty having run out some time ago, I forget exactly when, is such that more and more I find myself spraying my hair with room freshener.

I know I speak for both of us when I express our gratitude to Burt Shevelove, who died in April of 1982. Presenting us with the challenge of writing our Plautine comedy, Burt initiated an experience that was as entertaining as it was educational, one that has been a source of pride and pleasure for over a quarter of a century.

I hope that none of what I've written here – how difficult it all was, how long the writing took – has in any way sounded like a complaint. If I have one at all it is that we finally *did* finish it, did at last put together all our self-created puzzles, did make our way out of the maddening mazes in which we seemed endlessly to entrap ourselves, that the day ultimately came when we had no choice but to say goodbye to all of the terribly hard work that had become such a source of joy.

Odd, that I should have that same feeling as I write this; once more reluctant to let go of the play, to give it up, to let it belong to the audience. But in the theatre that passes for my mind, I hear the orchestra tuning up, I see the comics in the wings rehearsing their leers, the courtesans practising their pouts.

Anyone for a comedy tonight?

17 September 1990

A FUNNY THING HAPPENED
ON THE WAY TO THE FORUM

A Funny Thing Happened on the Way to the Forum was first
presented by Harold Prince at the Alvin Theatre, New York City,
on 8 May 1962 for 971 performances, with the following cast:

PROLOGUS	Zero Mostel
THE PROTEANS Eddie Phillips, George Reeder, David Evans	
SENEX, *a citizen of Rome*	David Burns
DOMINA, *his wife*	Ruth Kobart
HERO, *his son*	Brian Davies
HYSTERIUM, *slave to Senex and Domina*	Jack Gilford
LYCUS, *a dealer in courtesans*	John Carradine
PSEUDOLUS, *slave to Hero*	Zero Mostel
TINTINABULA	Roberta Keith
PANACEA	Lucienne Bridou
THE GEMINAE	Lisa James, Judy Alexander
VIBRATA	Myrna White
GYMNASIA	Gloria Kristy
PHILIA	Preshy Marker
ERRONIUS, *a citizen of Rome*	Raymond Walburn
MILES GLORIOSUS, *a warrior*	Ronald Holgate

Production Directed by George Abbott
Choreography and Musical Staging by Jack Cole
Settings and Costumes by Tony Walton
Lighting by Jean Rosenthal
Orchestrations by Irwin Kostal *and* Sid Ramin
Musical Direction by Harold Hastings
Dance Arrangements by Hal Schaefer

A Funny Thing Happened on the Way to the Forum was first presented in London by Harold Prince, Tony Walton and Richard Pilbrow, by arrangement with Send Manor Trust Ltd., at the Strand Theatre on 3 October 1963 for 762 performances, with the following cast:

PROLOGUS	Frankie Howerd
THE PROTEANS	Ben Aris, George Giles, Malcolm Macdonald
SENEX, *a citizen of Rome*	'Monsewer' Eddie Gray
DOMINA, *his wife*	Linda Gray
HERO, *his son*	John Rye
HYSTERIUM, *slave to Senex and Domina*	Kenneth Connor
PSEUDOLUS, *slave to Hero*	Frankie Howerd
LYCUS, *a dealer in courtesans*	Jon Pertwee
TINTINABULA	Norma Dunbar
PANACEA	Christine Child
THE GEMINAE	Marion Horton, Vyvyan Dunbar
VIBRATA	Faye Craig
GYMNASIA	Sula Freeman
PHILIA	Isla Blair
ERRONIUS, *a citizen of Rome*	Robertson Hare
MILES GLORIOSUS, *a warrior*	Leon Greene

Production Directed by George Abbott
Musical Numbers originally staged by Jack Cole
   re-staged by George Martin
Settings and Costumes by Tony Walton
Lighting by Jean Rosenthal
Orchestrations by Irwin Kostal *and* Sid Ramin
Musical Direction by Alyn Ainsworth
Dance Arrangements by Hal Schaefer

A Funny Thing Happened on the Way to the Forum was revived in the Olivier auditorium of the National Theatre, London, on 9 July 2004 (previews from 28 June), with the following cast:

PROLOGUS   Desmond Barrit
THE PROTEANS   Darren Carnall, Peter Caulfield,
                                              David Lucas. Graham MacDuff,
                                        Michael Rouse, Matthew Wolfenden
SENEX, *an old man*   Sam Kelly
DOMINA, *his wife*   Isla Blair
HERO, *his son*   Vince Leigh
HYSTERIUM, *slave to Senex and Dominia*   Hamish McColl
PSEUDOLUS, *slave to Hero*   Desmond Barrit
LYCUS, *a buyer and seller of courtesans*   David Schneider
TINTINABULA, *a courtesan*   Jane Fowler
PANACEA, *a courtesan*   Lorraine Stewart
THE GEMINAE, *courtesans*   Simone De La Rue,
                                                            Hayley Newton
VIBRATA, *a courtesan*   Michelle Lukes
GYMNASIA, *a courtesan*   Tiffany Graves
PHILIA, *a virgin*   Caroline Sheen
ERRONIUS, *an old man*   Harry Towb
MILES GLORIOSUS, *a warrior*   Philip Quast
SERGEANT   Alan Leith
SWINGS   Owain Rhys Davies, Sarah O'Gleby,
                                                        Spencer Soloman

Other parts played by members of the Company

Directed by Edward Hall
Choreographed by Rob Ashford
Set Designed by Julian Crouch
Costumes Designed by Kevin Pollard
Orchestrations by Michael Starobin
Musical Direction and Dance Arrangements by Martin Lowe
Lighting Designed by Paul Anderson
Sound Designed by Paul Groothuis

Musical Numbers

Act One

'Comedy Tonight'	PROLOGUS, PROTEANS, COMPANY
'Love, I Hear'	HERO
'Free'	PSEUDOLUS, HERO
'The House of Marcus Lycus'	LYCUS, PSEUDOLUS, COURTESANS
'Lovely'	HERO, PHILIA
'Pretty Little Picture'	PSEUDOLUS, HERO, PHILIA
'Everybody Ought to Have a Maid'	SENEX, PSEUDOLUS, HYSTERIUM, LYCUS
'I'm Calm'	HYSTERIUM
'Impossible'	SENEX, HERO
'Bring Me My Bride'	MILES, PSEUDOLUS, COURTESANS, PROTEANS

Act Two

'That Dirty Old Man'	DOMINA
'That'll Show Him'	PHILIA
'Lovely'	PSEUDOLUS, HYSTERIUM
Funeral Sequence and Dance	PSEUDOLUS, MILES, COURTESANS, PROTEANS
'Comedy Tonight'	COMPANY

Characters

PROLOGUS, *an actor*
THE PROTEANS
SENEX, *an old man*
DOMINA, *his wife*
HERO, *his son, in love with Philia*
HYSTERIUM, *slave to Senex and Domina*
PSEUDOLUS, *slave to Hero*
LYCUS, *a buyer and seller of courtesans*
TINTINABULA, *a courtesan*
PANACEA, *a courtesan*
THE GEMINAE, *courtesans*
VIBRATA, *a courtesan*
GYMNASIA, *a courtesan*
PHILIA, *a virgin*
ERRONIUS, *an old man*
MILES GLORIOSUS, *a warrior*

Time   *Two hundred years before the Christian era, a day in spring.*

Place   *A street in Rome in front of the houses of Erronius, Senex, and Lycus.*

Authors' Note   *This is a scenario for vaudevillians. There are many details omitted from the script. They are part of any comedian's bag of tricks: the double take, the mad walk, the sighs, the smirks, the stammerings. All these and more are intended to be supplied by the actor and you, the reader.*

ACT ONE

PROLOGUS *enters through traveller, salutes audience, addresses them.*

PROLOGUS. Playgoers, I bid you welcome. The theatre is a temple, and we are here to worship the gods of comedy and tragedy. Tonight, I am pleased to announce a comedy. We shall employ every device we know in our desire to divert you.

During this scene, there are musical interludes during which PROLOGUS *and the* PROTEANS *do various bits of pantomime and general clowning, using a prop leg.* PROLOGUS *gestures to orchestra, sings.*

Something familiar,
Something peculiar,
Something for everyone – a comedy tonight!
Something appealing,
Something appalling,
Something for everyone – a comedy tonight!
Nothing with kings,
Nothing with crowns,
Bring on the lovers, liars and clowns!
Old situations,
New complications,
Nothing portentous or polite:
Tragedy tomorrow,
Comedy tonight!

During the following, he brings on the three PROTEANS.

Something familiar,
Something peculiar,
Something for everyone – a comedy tonight!
Something appealing,
Something appalling,
Something for everyone – a comedy tonight!

PROTEANS.
Tragedy tomorrow –

PROLOGUS.
Comedy tonight!
Something convulsive,
Something repulsive,
Something for everyone –

ALL.
A comedy tonight!

PROLOGUS.
Something aesthetic,

PROTEANS.
Something frenetic,

PROLOGUS.
Something for everyone –

ALL.
A comedy tonight!

PROTEANS.
Nothing with gods,
Nothing with fate.

PROLOGUS.
Weighty affairs will just have to wait.

PROTEANS.
Nothing that's formal,

PROLOGUS.
Nothing that's normal,

ALL.
No recitations to recite!
Open up the curtain –

The traveller parts halfway, then closes as if by accident, causing confusion. After a moment, it reopens completely, revealing a street in Rome. Stage centre stands the house of SENEX; *on either side, the houses of* LYCUS *and* ERRONIUS. SENEX's *house is hidden behind another curtain.*

PROLOGUS.
Comedy tonight!

Speaks.

It all takes place on a street in Rome, around and about these three houses.

Indicates ERRONIUS*'s house.*

First, the house of Erronius, a befuddled old man abroad now in search of his children, stolen in infancy by pirates.

Sings.

Something for everyone – a comedy tonight!

The PROTEANS *appear in the upper window of the house and pantomime.*

Something erratic,
Something dramatic,
Something for everyone – a comedy tonight!
Frenzy and frolic,
Strictly symbolic,
Something for everyone – a comedy tonight!

Speaks, indicating LYCUS*'s house.*

Second, the house of Lycus, a buyer and seller of the flesh of beautiful women. That's for those of you who have absolutely no interest in pirates.

Sings.

Something for everyone – a comedy tonight!

PROTEANS *dance in front of the house; one of them disappears into the floor.* PROLOGUS *reacts, then continues, speaking.*

Raise the curtain!

Inner curtain drops into floor.

And finally, the house of Senex, who lives here with his wife and son. Also in this house lives Pseudolus, slave to the son. Pseudolus is probably my favourite character in the piece. A role of enormous variety and nuance, and played by an actor of such . . . let me put it this way . . . *I* play the part.

Sings.

Anything you ask for – comedy tonight!

PROTEANS *re-enter.*

And these are the Proteans, only three, yet they do the work of thirty. They are difficult to recognise in the many parts they play. Watch them closely.

PROTEANS *appear in and out of* SENEX'*s house in assorted costumes as* PROLOGUS *comments.*

A proud Roman. A patrician Roman. A pretty Roman. A Roman slave. A Roman soldier.

PROTEAN *appears with crude wooden ladder.*

A Roman ladder.

PROTEAN *enters, juggling.*

Tremendous skill!

He juggles badly. PROTEAN *enters.*

Incredible versatility!

He fumbles in changing wigs. PROTEAN *enters with gong.*

And, above all, dignity!

He strikes gong, his skirt falls.

And now, the entire company!

The company enters from SENEX'*s house and forms a line.*

ALL (*sing*).
  Something familiar,
  Something peculiar,
  Something for everybody – comedy tonight!

STAGE RIGHT.
  Something that's gaudy,

STAGE LEFT.
  Something that's bawdy,

PROLOGUS.
  Something for everybawdy –

ALL.
  Comedy tonight!

MILES.
  Nothing that's grim,

DOMINA.
Nothing that's Greek!

PROLOGUS (*leading* GYMNASIA *centre*).
She plays Medea later this week.

ALL.
Stunning surprises,
Cunning disguises,
Hundreds of actors out of sight!

ERRONIUS.
Pantaloons and tunics!

SENEX.
Courtesans and eunuchs!

DOMINA.
Funerals and chases!

LYCUS.
Baritones and basses!

PHILIA.
Panderers!

HERO.
Philanderers!

HYSTERIUM.
Cupidity!

MILES.
Timidity!

LYCUS.
Mistakes!

ERRONIUS.
Fakes!

PHILIA.
Rhymes!

DOMINA.
Mimes!

PROLOGUS.
Tumblers!
Grumblers!

Fumblers!
Bumblers!

ALL.
No royal curse,
No Trojan horse,
And a happy ending, of course!
Goodness and badness,
Man in his madness,
This time it all turns out all right!
Tragedy tomorrow!
Comedy tonight!
One – two – three!

All exit, except PROLOGUS.

PROLOGUS (*addresses the heavens*). Oh, Thespis, we place ourselves in your hands.

To audience.

The play begins.

Exits.

Music up. PHILIA *appears at window of* LYCUS*'s house and* HERO *appears on balcony of* SENEX*'s house.* SENEX *enters from his house.*

SENEX (*calls*). Slaves!

PHILIA *exits, as* PROTEANS *enter from* SENEX*'s house, dressed as* SLAVES, *assume slavish attitudes.*

We are about to start our journey. My robe!

PROTEANS *place robe on him.*

My wreath.

PROTEANS *place wreath on his head.*

DOMINA (*appearing in doorway of* SENEX'*s house*). Senex!

SENEX (*frowns*). My wife.

DOMINA. Slaves! Stop cringing and fetch the baggage!

PROTEANS (*exiting into* SENEX*'s house*). Yes, yes, yes.

DOMINA. Senex, you are master of the house and no help at all. Where is Pseudolus? Where is Hysterium? Summon them!

SENEX *is about to speak,* DOMINA *calls out.*

Pseudolus! Hysterium!

HYSTERIUM *enters from* SENEX*'s house. During the following,* SENEX *drifts toward* LYCUS*'s house.*

HYSTERIUM. Ah, madam, you called?

DOMINA. Yes, Hysterium.

HYSTERIUM. And I answered. Ever your humble. (*Kisses hem of her cape.*)

DOMINA. Have you prepared my potions?

HYSTERIUM (*holds up small bag*). Yes, madam. In addition to your usual potions, I have included one for tantrums and one for queasiness.

DOMINA. Thank you, Hysterium, slave of slaves.

HYSTERIUM. I live to grovel.

Kisses her hem. DOMINA *calls to* HERO *on balcony of* SENEX*'s house.*

DOMINA. Hero, come kiss your mother goodbye.

HERO. Yes, mother.

Exits into SENEX*'s house.* SLAVES *re-enter, carrying baggage.*

DOMINA. Slaves, take that baggage and go before us, you clumsies!

PROTEANS (*as they scurry off*). Yes, yes, clumsies, yes.

DOMINA. Senex! Come away from that house of shame!

SENEX (*crossing to her*). I was just standing there saying, 'Shame, shame, shame!'

DOMINA. Hysterium!

HYSTERIUM. Yes, madam?

DOMINA. Where is Pseudolus?

HYSTERIUM. Where is he indeed! I have not seen him since he dressed Hero this morning.

DOMINA. Tell him that while we are gone, he is to watch over

Hero. He is to keep him cheerful, well fed, and far from the opposite sex.

SENEX. My dear, the boy has to learn sometime.

DOMINA. And when that time comes, *you* shall tell him . . .

SENEX. Yes, dear.

DOMINA. . . . . what little you know. Now, go and fetch the gift we bring my mother.

SENEX. Yes, dear.

Exits into his house, as HERO *enters from it.*

HERO. Good morning, father.

DOMINA. Ah, Hero. Your father and I are off to visit my mother in the country. What a joy it would be were you to accompany us. But, alas, the sight of anyone in good health fills my mother with rage.

SENEX re-enters carrying a bust of DOMINA.

Ah, there I am. Do you think it will please my mother?

HYSTERIUM. Oh, yes, madam. The craftsmanship is superb.

DOMINA. And the resemblance?

HYSTERIUM. Frightening.

DOMINA. The time of farewell is at hand. Hysterium, slave in-chief, here are my husband's final instructions.

SENEX opens his mouth to speak, she continues.

In his absence, his entire household is in your spotless care. Your word shall be absolute, your authority unquestioned.

SENEX. And furthermore –

DOMINA. We are on our way!

SENEX (*mutters*). We are on our way.

DOMINA. Farewell, beloved son. Farewell, thoughtful Hysterium. Senex, come along! And carry my bust with pride.

Exits. A beat, and then her voice is heard.

Senex!

SENEX. Yes, dear. (*To audience.*) A lesson for you all. Never fall in love during a total eclipse!

Exits.

HYSTERIUM (*to audience*). Well, to work, to work! Now that I am completely in charge, I am going to be a very busy slave.

Sees HERO, *who has drifted toward* LYCUS'*s house.*

Here! Come away from there. You must never know what goes on in that house.

HERO. But I do know.

HYSTERIUM. You do?

HERO *nods.*

Isn't it amazing? Well, I can't stand here talking.

Goes to SENEX'*s house, picks something from a column, stamps it out, grimaces, enters house, calling.*

Pseudolus!

HERO *watches him go, then turns to audience.*

HERO (*sings*).
Now that we're alone,
May I tell you
I've been feeling very strange?
Either something's in the air
Or else a change
Is happening in me.
I think I know the cause,
I hope I know the cause.
From everything I've heard,
There's only one cause it can be . . .

Love, I hear,
Makes you sigh a lot.
Also, love, I hear,
Leaves you weak.
Love, I hear,
Makes you blush
And turns you ashen.
You try to speak with passion

And squeak,
I hear.

Love, they say,
Makes you pine away,
But you pine away
With an idiotic grin.
I pine, I blush,
I squeak, I squawk.
Today I woke
Too weak to walk.
What's love, I hear,
I feel . . . I fear . . .
I'm in.

Sighs.

See what I mean?
Da-da-da-da-da-da-da . . .
(I hum a lot, too.)
I'm dazed, I'm pale,
I'm sick, I'm sore;
I've never felt so well before!
What's love, I hear,
I feel . . . I fear . . .
I know I am . . .
I'm sure . . . I mean . . .
I think . . . I trust . . .
I pray . . . I must . . .
Be in!

Forgive me if I shout . . .
Forgive me if I crow . . .
I've only just found out
And, well . . .
I thought you ought to know.

PROTEANS *enter dressed as* CITIZENS, *holding*
PSEUDOLUS *by the arms. They utter obviously fake
chatter.*

HERO. Pseudolus!

FIRST CITIZEN (*salutes*). Citizen! This is your slave? He was
parading as a citizen.

PSEUDOLUS. Believe me, master, I was not parading. This is parading. (*Demonstrates.*) *I* was walking.

Starts to walk off. CITIZEN *stops him.*

SECOND CITIZEN. Come back here!

THIRD CITIZEN (*to* HERO). He invited us to game with him, and, in a matter of moments, he had taken all our money.

FIRST CITIZEN. He was using weighted dice!

HERO (*to* PSEUDOLUS). Return the money.

SECOND CITIZEN. He took nine minae.

PSEUDOLUS. Nine?! I took seven!

HERO. Give them nine.

PSEUDOLUS (*handing coins to* CITIZEN). One, two, three, four . . . I am being cheated out of the money I won fairly.

HERO. Pseudolus!

PSEUDOLUS (*giving* CITIZENS *coins*). Seven, eight.

FIRST CITIZEN. What happened to five and six?

HERO *glares at* PSEUDOLUS.

PSEUDOLUS. I'm coming to them. Nine, five, six! (*Hands them three more coins.*)

SECOND CITIZEN. Come, fellow citizens!

CITIZENS *exit, chattering.*

PSEUDOLUS (*sheepishly*). I should be whipped . . . gently. But I only did it for money. I thought if I could raise enough you'd let me buy my freedom from you.

HERO. Oh, Pseudolus, not again!

PSEUDOLUS. It's all I think about. I hate being a slave.

HERO. Better a slave than a slave to love.

PSEUDOLUS. That's easy for you to . . . Love? You? Tell me, master, who is she? Anyone I know?

HERO. Sometimes you can see her through that window. (*Points to* LYCUS's *house.*)

PSEUDOLUS. Through that win – (*Horrified.*) A courtesan in the house of Lycus? Your parents would be outraged if they could hear you.

HERO. I don't care!

PSEUDOLUS. Do you know how many minae a girl like that would cost?

HERO. And worth every drachma! Oh, Pseudolus, I would give anything for her.

PSEUDOLUS. You would? You really love this girl?

HERO *sighs.*

I like the way you said that. Now, you cannot afford to buy this girl, but in spite of that, suppose someone, someone with tremendous cunning and guile, could arrange for her to be yours.

HERO. Yes?

PSEUDOLUS. If that someone could arrange it, what would you give me?

HERO. Everything!

PSEUDOLUS. Everything? What do you own? Twenty minae, a collection of seashells and me.

HERO. Right.

PSEUDOLUS. You don't have to give me the twenty minae, or the seashells. If I get you that girl, just give me me.

HERO. Give you you?

PSEUDOLUS. My freedom.

HERO. Pseudolus! People do not go about freeing slaves.

PSEUDOLUS. Be the first! Start a fashion!

HERO (*a pause, then*). Get me that girl!

PSEUDOLUS. And if I can?

HERO. You are free!

PSEUDOLUS. I am what?

HERO. Free!

PSEUDOLUS. Free!

Sings.

Oh, what a word!
Oh, what a word!

Speaks.

Say it again!

HERO. Free!

PSEUDOLUS (*sings*).
I've often thought,
I've often dreamed
How it would be . . .
And yet I never thought I'd be . . .

Speaks.

Once more.

HERO. Free!

PSEUDOLUS (*sings*).
But when you come to think of such things . . .
A man should have the rights that all others . . .
Can you imagine
What it will be like when I am . . .
Can you see me?

Can you see me as a Roman with my head unbowed?
(Sing it good and loud . . .)

HERO.
Free!

PSEUDOLUS.
Like a Roman, having rights
And like a Roman, proud!
Can you see me?

HERO.
I can see you!

PSEUDOLUS.
Can you see me as a voter fighting graft and vice?
(Sing it soft and nice . . .)

HERO.
Free.

PSEUDOLUS.
  Why, I'll be so conscientious that I may vote twice!
  Can you see me?
  Can you see me?

  When I'm free to be whatever I want to be,
  Think what wonders I'll accomplish then!
  When the master that I serve is me and just me,

  Can you see me being equal with my countrymen?
  Can you see me being Pseudolus the Citizen?
  Can you see me being . . . ?
  Give it to me once again!

HERO.
  Free!

PSEUDOLUS.
  That's it!

HERO.
  Free!

PSEUDOLUS.
  Yes!

HERO.
  Fr . . .

PSEUDOLUS (*claps his hand over* HERO's *mouth*).
  Now, not so fast!
  I didn't think . . .
  The way I am,
  I have a roof,
  Three meals a day,
  And I don't have to pay a thing . . .
  I'm just a slave and everything's free.
  If I were free,
  Then nothing would be free,
  And if I'm beaten now and then,
  What does it matter?

HERO (*softly, seductively*).
  Free.

PSEUDOLUS (*brightening*).
  Can you see me?

Can you see me as a poet writing poetry?
All my verse will be . . .

HERO.

Free!

PSEUDOLUS.

A museum will have me pickled for posterity!
Can you see me?

HERO (*with a grimace*).

I can see you!

PSEUDOLUS.

Can you see me as a lover, one of great renown,
Women falling down?

HERO.

Free?

PSEUDOLUS.

No,
But I'll buy the house of Lycus for my house in town.
Can you see me?
Can't you see me?

Be you anything from king to baker of cakes,
You're a vegetable unless you're free!
It's a little word, but oh, the difference it makes:
It's the necessary essence of democracy,
It's the thing that every slave should have the right to be,
And I soon will have the right to buy a slave for me!
Can you see him?
Well, I'll free him!

When a Pseudolus can move, the universe shakes,
But I'll never move until I'm free!
Such a little word, but oh, the difference it makes:
I'll be Pseudolus the founder of a family,
I'll be Pseudolus the pillar of society,
I'll be Pseudolus the man, if I can only be . . .

HERO.

Free!

PSEUDOLUS.

Sing it!

HERO.
  Free!

PSEUDOLUS.
  Spell it!

HERO.
  F-r-double . . .

PSEUDOLUS.
  No, the long way . . .

HERO.
  F-R-E-E

BOTH.
  FREE!!!

  LYCUS *enters from his house, calls into it.*

LYCUS. What a day! What a day! Come out here!

  PROTEAN, *dressed as* EUNUCH, *enters from house,*
  holding fan.

  What do you think you are doing, eunuch? I have told you a
  thousand times not to fan the girls while they're still wet!
  You'll never learn. You'll be a eunuch all your life!

  EUNUCH *exits into house.* LYCUS *turns to audience.*

  What a day! I have to go to the Senate this morning. I'm
  blackmailing one of the Senators.

  Starts off, as PSEUDOLUS *whispers to* HERO.

PSEUDOLUS. Quick! Your money bag!

  HERO *hands him money bag.*

  Good morning, Lycus.

  Jingles money bag behind LYCUS*'s back.* LYCUS *stops.*

LYCUS. I know that sound, and I love it.

  Turns to PSEUDOLUS.

  Is that money?

PSEUDOLUS. What do you think?

LYCUS. How did you come to all this?

PSEUDOLUS. An unexpected legacy. My uncle Simo, the noted Carthaginian elephant breeder, came to an untimely end. He was crushed to death on the last day of the mating season. This morning I bought my freedom.

LYCUS. Congratulations!

PSEUDOLUS. With this much left over for one gross indulgence.

LYCUS. Good.

PSEUDOLUS. Lycus, I am now in the market for a lifetime companion. Tell me, have you anything lying about in there, anything to satisfy an Olympian appetite?

LYCUS. Pseudolus, friend and *citizen*, I have travelled the world in search of beauty, and I can say with modesty that I have the finest assortment in Rome.

PSEUDOLUS. Show me.

LYCUS *claps his hands.*

LYCUS. Eunuchs! A buyer!

EUNUCHS *enter from* LYCUS*'s house, drape banner over door.* PSEUDOLUS *sits on stool.* LYCUS *sings.*

There is merchandise for every need
At the house of Marcus Lycus.
All the merchandise is guaranteed
At the house of Marcus Lycus.
For a sense of sensuality
Or an opulence thereof,
Patronise the house of Marcus Lycus,
Merchant of love.

For your most assured approval and your more than possible purchase, here are the fruits of my search. Behold . . . Tintinabula.

TINTINABULA *enters from behind banner, poses.*

Out of the East, with the face of an idol . . . the arms of a willow tree . . . and the pelvis of a camel.

She dances. PSEUDOLUS *looks at* HERO, *who shakes his head no.*

PSEUDOLUS (*to* LYCUS). Don't you have anyone in there a bit less . . . noisy?

LYCUS. I have. May I present Panacea.

PANACEA *enters.*

To make her available to you, I outbid the King of Nubia. Panacea, with a face that holds a thousand promises, and a body that stands behind each promise.

PANACEA *dances.* HERO *shakes his head no.*
PSEUDOLUS *looks* PANACEA *over, yawns.*

You are disturbed?

PSEUDOLUS. The proportions. Don't misunderstand me. (*Spreading his hands before her bosom.*) I love the breadth. It's the length. She may be the right length, but is it right for me? You see what I mean.

Stands with her, back-to-back.

Isn't she a bit too short?

LYCUS. Definitely not.

PSEUDOLUS (*wiggles, then*). Too tall?

LYCUS. No. Like that you look perfect together.

PSEUDOLUS. Yes, but how often will we find ourselves in this position? (*Turns to face her.*) Perhaps if we . . .

LYCUS. No need to compromise. Consider the Geminae.

GEMINAE *enter.*

A matched pair.

They dance.

Either one a divinely assembled woman, together an infinite number of mathematical possibilities. They are flawless.

HERO *shakes his head no.*

PSEUDOLUS. I quite agree. But I am a man of limited means and I don't suppose you'd break up a set.

LYCUS. I couldn't. You understand.

PSEUDOLUS. Completely.

LYCUS. Fortunately, we still have . . . Vibrata.

VIBRATA *enters.*

Exotic as a desert bloom . . . wondrous as a flamingo . . . lithe as a tigress . . . for the man whose interest is wild life . . .

VIBRATA *sings, dances.* HERO *shakes his head no.* PSEUDOLUS *goes to* VIBRATA.

PSEUDOLUS. Lycus, all that I can see is a sight to behold, but I keep feeling there is something wrong. Perhaps a cleft palate, a hammer toe . . .

LYCUS. Wait. I know exactly what you want. May I present . . . Gymnasia.

GYMNASIA *enters, does bump.* PSEUDOLUS *falls off stool.* HERO *shakes his head no, but* PSEUDOLUS *is completely captivated.*

Gymnasia, a giant stage on which a thousand dramas can be played.

PSEUDOLUS *circles her, stops behind her, gestures to* LYCUS.

PSEUDOLUS. Lycus, could I see you back here a moment?

LYCUS *disappears behind* GYMNASIA. *He and* PSEUDOLUS *gesture.* PSEUDOLUS *steps into the clear.*

Two hundred minae?! For what?!

LYCUS. Figure it out for yourself.

PSEUDOLUS. Yes, it is a fair price by the pound. But what disturbs me, frankly, is the upkeep. Perhaps you would have more success selling her to some fraternal organisation. A group dedicated to good works. But on the other hand . . . (*Puts his head on her bosom.*)

HERO. Pseudolus!

PSEUDOLUS. Yes, darling?

HERO (*pulls him aside*). Do you want your freedom?

PSEUDOLUS (*looks back at* GYMNASIA). More than ever. (*To* LYCUS.) May I see the next girl?

LYCUS. That is the entire lot. Surely there is one among these to satisfy you.

PSEUDOLUS. As yet I have not seen exactly what I had in mind.

LYCUS (*claps hands*). Courtesans! Out of the sun and into the house. I shall return in time to lead you in midday prayers.

> COURTESANS *and* EUNUCHS *exit.* PHILIA's *head appears in upper window of* LYCUS's *house.*

HERO (*whispers to* PSEUDOLUS). Pseudolus, there she is!

PSEUDOLUS (*to* LYCUS). Oh, you fox! 'That is the entire lot.' Did I not just spy a golden head and a pair of sky blue eyes? A body clad in flowing white?

LYCUS. Oh, that one. A recent arrival from Crete. A virgin.

PSEUDOLUS (*nudging* HERO). A virgin.

HERO. A virgin!

PSEUDOLUS (*to* LYCUS). Well??

LYCUS. Only yesterday she was sold.

HERO. Sold!

> *Draws his dagger melodramatically.* PSEUDOLUS *wrests it from him.*

PSEUDOLUS. Behave yourself! (*Begins casually cleaning his nails with dagger.*) She was sold?

LYCUS. To the great captain, Miles Gloriosus, who comes this day to claim her. She cost five hundred minae.

PSEUDOLUS (*amazed*). Five hundred!

LYCUS. A great sum, to be sure. But being a man of conquest, his heart was set on a virgin.

PSEUDOLUS. You say she just arrived from Crete?

LYCUS. Yes.

PSEUDOLUS. Mmm. I hope the great captain is kind to her. She deserves a bit of affection before . . . (*Sighs, then to* HERO.) Tragic, is it not?

> HERO *moans.*

LYCUS. What is tragic?

PSEUDOLUS. The news from Crete.

LYCUS. What news?

PSEUDOLUS. Why should I darken your day? Farewell, Lycus.

LYCUS (*grabs him*). What is the news?

PSEUDOLUS. What news?

LYCUS. The news from Crete.

PSEUDOLUS. I heard it. Tragic.

LYCUS. Pseudolus! (*Shakes him.*)

PSEUDOLUS. You force me to tell you! Crete is ravaged by a great plague. People are dying by the thousands.

LYCUS. But this girl is healthy. She goes smiling through the day.

PSEUDOLUS. She doesn't! I thought you knew. When they start to smile, the end is near.

LYCUS. No!

PSEUDOLUS. Yes. I am told it is lovely now in Crete. Everyone lying there, smiling.

LYCUS. Is it contagious?

PSEUDOLUS. Did you ever see a plague that wasn't?

LYCUS. My other girls!

PSEUDOLUS. You had best get her out of there.

HERO. Yes!

LYCUS. And then?

PSEUDOLUS. I could look after her until the captain comes.

HERO. He could!

LYCUS. But would *you* not be . . . ?

PSEUDOLUS. I have already had the plague. I would tell you about it but . . .

Pantomimes disgust.

LYCUS. I do hope she lives until the captain gets here. (*Exits into his house.*)

HERO (*elated*). Pseudolus, I am to be with her!

PSEUDOLUS. Until the captain arrives.

HERO (*sadly*). Yes.

PSEUDOLUS. Wait! (*Thinks a moment.*)

HERO. Yes?

PSEUDOLUS. A brilliant idea!

HERO. Yes?

PSEUDOLUS. That's what we have to find. A brilliant idea.

HERO. You must find one.

LYCUS (*speaking into his house as he backs out of it*). Come, come, my dear. This way. Don't touch that pillar. Here is someone I want you to meet.

PHILIA *enters from house, carrying a bag.*

Philia, this is Pseudolus. You are to stay with him until the captain comes. It will not be long. (*Aside to* PSEUDOLUS.) Pseudolus! Thank you, Pseudolus. If none in the house were to your liking, there will soon be new arrivals. You shall have first choice, because, Pseudolus, you are a friend. (*Bows.*)

PSEUDOLUS (*returning the bow*). And you, Lycus, are a gentleman and a procurer.

LYCUS *exits.* HERO *and* PHILIA *stand staring at each other.* PSEUDOLUS *looks at them, then turns to audience.*

There they are. Together. And I must keep them that way, together, if I am to be free. What to do? What to do? (*To himself.*) I need help. I'll go to the harbour. There I may find a way out! I am off! The captain!

HERO *and* PHILIA *turn to him, alarmed.*

Watch for him. He may arrive this way . . .

PHILIA *turns from* HERO, *looks off.*

. . . or he may arrive this way.

HERO *turns, looks off.*

No, no. You watch this way.

Turns PHILIA *around.*

And you watch that way.

Turns HERO *around.* HERO *and* PHILIA *now face each other.*

Much better. (*Starts to exit, stops, addresses audience.*) Don't worry. Nothing will happen. He's a virgin, too. (*Runs off.*)

PHILIA. My name is Philia.

HERO. Yes.

PHILIA. I do not know your name, but you have beautiful legs.

HERO. My name is Hero and . . . uh . . . you have beautiful legs . . . I imagine.

PHILIA. I would show them to you, but they are sold.

HERO. I know.

PHILIA. Along with the rest of me. I cost five hundred minae. Is that a lot of money?

HERO. Oh, yes.

PHILIA. More than three hundred?

HERO. Nearly twice as much.

PHILIA. Those are the two numbers that mix me up, three and five. I hope that captain doesn't expect me to do a lot of adding.

HERO. You can't add?

PHILIA. We are taught beauty and grace, and no more. I cannot add, or spell, or anything. I have but one talent.

Sings.

I'm lovely,
All I am is lovely,
Lovely is the one thing I can do.
Winsome,
What I am is winsome,
Radiant as in some
Dream come true.
Oh,

Isn't it a shame?
I can neither sew
Nor cook nor read nor write my name.
But I'm happy
Merely being lovely,
For it's one thing I can give to you.

HERO. Philia . . .

PHILIA. Yes?

HERO. Say my name.

PHILIA. Just say your name?

HERO. Yes.

PHILIA. Very well. (*A blank look.*) I have forgotten it.

HERO (*disappointed*). It's Hero.

PHILIA. Forgive me, Hero. I have no memory for names.

HERO. You don't need one. You don't need anything.

Sings.

You're lovely,
Absolutely lovely,
Who'd believe the loveliness of you?
Winsome,
Sweet and warm and winsome,
Radiant as in some
Dream come true.

PHILIA.
True!

HERO.
Now
Venus would seem tame,
Helen and her thou-
Sand ships would have to die of shame.

BOTH.
And I'm happy,
Happy that you're (I'm) lovely,
For there's one thing loveliness can do:
It's a gift for me to share with you!

They kiss.

HERO. Do you know? I've never been kissed before.

PHILIA. That's the very first thing they teach us.

HERO. Philia . . . I love you.

PHILIA. And I love you.

They embrace, as HYSTERIUM *enters from* SENEX's *house, muttering.*

HYSTERIUM. Pseudolus! Where is that – ?

Sees HERO *and* PHILIA.

Oh, no! No, no, no, no!

HERO (*frightened*). Hysterium – this is Philia.

HYSTERIUM. Never mind who she is, who is she? Where is she from?

HERO (*haltingly*). She is from the house of Lycus.

HYSTERIUM. A courtesan!

PHILIA. I am a virgin.

HYSTERIUM (*disbelievingly, with a fake smile*). Of course. Hero, this will never do. Never, never. Bid farewell to this young lady so that she can go about her . . . uh . . . business.

HERO. But Pseudolus said . . .

HYSTERIUM. Pseudolus! I might have known!

PSEUDOLUS *runs on.*

PSEUDOLUS (*spots* HYSTERIUM, *then to* HERO). Hero! Master!

HYSTERIUM. Pseudolus!

PSEUDOLUS *reacts, polishes pillar of house.*

Pseudolus!

PSEUDOLUS. Yes, Hysterium?

HYSTERIUM. Pseudolus!

PSEUDOLUS. Pronounced perfectly! You know, a lot of people say *P*seudolus, and I hate it. (*Aside to* HERO.) Show the girl our garden.

HERO *and* PHILIA *exit behind* SENEX's *house.*

HYSTERIUM. How dare you! Arranging an assignation between an innocent boy and a you-know-what!

PSEUDOLUS (*stopping him*). Hysterium, there is something you should know about that you-know-what.

HYSTERIUM. What?

PSEUDOLUS. That girl, about whom you think the worst, is my daughter.

HYSTERIUM. Your what?

PSEUDOLUS. My daughter. You've heard me speak of her.

HYSTERIUM. Never!

PSEUDOLUS. Well, I don't like to talk about her. (*Polishes pillar.*)

HYSTERIUM. That girl is not your daughter.

PSEUDOLUS. My sister?

HYSTERIUM. I shall go tell his parents.

PSEUDOLUS. Wait! Hysterium, the truth. She has been sold to a captain who comes any moment now to claim her.

HYSTERIUM. Oh. I go tell his parents!

PSEUDOLUS. I go with you!

HYSTERIUM. You don't want to be there when I tell them about you!

PSEUDOLUS. No, I want *you* to be there when I tell them about *you*!

HYSTERIUM. Tell them *what* about me? I have nothing to fear. I am a pillar of virtue. I go.

Starts to leave, PSEUDOLUS *stops him.*

PSEUDOLUS. I think it might be of interest to the family that their slave-in-chief, their pillar of virtue, has secreted within the confines of his cubicle Rome's most extensive and diversified collection of erotic pottery.

HYSTERIUM *freezes in horror.*

HYSTERIUM. Pseudolus! (*Calls out.*) Hero!

PSEUDOLUS. Tell me, where did you ever get that fruit bowl
with the frieze of . . . ? (*Indicates an erotic pose or two.*)

HYSTERIUM. Pseudolus!

HERO *and* PHILIA *enter.*

Hero, as you know, your mother and father placed me in
charge of your innocence. However, I have decided to allow
you to remain with the girl until the arrival of her captain.

HERO. Oh, Philia!

Embraces her.

HYSTERIUM. Here! Stop doing that!

Separates them.

You could hurt each other! (*Exiting into* SENEX's *house.*)
Ohhhhh!

PSEUDOLUS. Master, I said we needed a brilliant idea.

HERO. Yes?

PSEUDOLUS. I have been to the harbour, and I have found
one. Come along!

PHILIA. Are we going somewhere?

PSEUDOLUS. *You* are. You have your belongings. (*To* HERO.)
Let us fetch yours.

HERO. Where are we to go?

PSEUDOLUS. Away.

HERO. *Where* away?

PSEUDOLUS. *Far* away!

HERO. But my family . . .

PHILIA. My captain . . .

PSEUDOLUS. There is only room for two of you.

HERO. Where?

PSEUDOLUS (*sings*).
    In the Tiber there sits a boat,
    Gently dipping its bow,
    Trim and tidy and built to float.
    Pretty little picture?

Now . . .
Put a boy on the starboard side,
Leaning out at the rail.
Next to him put a blushing bride,
Slim and slender and starry-eyed.
Down below put a tiny bed.
The sun gets pale,
The sea gets red,
And off they sail
On the first high tide,
The boat and the bed and the boy and the bride!

It's a pretty little picture, oh, my!
Pretty little picture, how true!
Pretty little picture which I,
Pseudolittlelus, give to you!

Feel the roll of the playful waves!
See the sails as they swell!
Hear the whips on the galley slaves!
Pretty little picture?
Well . . .
Let it carry your cares away,
Out of sight, out of mind,
Past the buoy and through the bay –
Soon there's nothing but sea and spray.
Night descends and the moon's aglow.
Your arms entwined,
You steal below,
And far behind
At the edge of day,
The bong of the bell of the buoy in the bay,
And the boat and the boy and the bride are away!

It's a pretty little picture to share
As the little boat sails to sea.
Take a little trip free as air,
Have a little freedom on me!

HERO *and* PHILIA.
No worries,
No bothers,
No captains,
No fathers!

PSEUDOLUS.

> In the ocean an island waits,
> Smooth and sandy and pink,
> Filled with lemons and nuts and dates.
> Pretty little picture?
> Think:
> In a cottage of cypress trees,
> Seashells dotting the door,
> Boy and bride live a life of ease,
> Doing nothing but what they please.
> And every night when the stars appear,
> There's nothing more
> To see or hear,
> There's just the shore
> Where the lovers lie,
> The sand and the sea and the stars and the sky,
> And the sound of a soft little satisfied sigh . . .

> HERO *and* PHILIA *sigh.*

ALL.

> All your petty little problems will cease,
> And your little blessings will flow,
> And your little family increase.
> Pretty little picture?

PSEUDOLUS.

> No, no!
> Pretty little masterpiece!

ALL.

> Pretty little picture!

PSEUDOLUS. Come! We go!

HERO. Yes!

PHILIA. Wait! I cannot go.

PSEUDOLUS. Why can you not?!

PHILIA. As long as the captain has a contract I must go with him. That is the way of a courtesan.

HERO. Oh, Venus, why did you bring us together, only to part us?

PHILIA. Be brave, Hero.

HERO. For us there will never be happiness.

PHILIA. We will have to learn to be happy without it.

PSEUDOLUS (*to audience*). Have you been listening? Do you believe this? And not a word about me or my freedom. (*Firmly.*) She *must* go with him!

PHILIA. This waiting out here is torture. Why doesn't he come and take me?

PSEUDOLUS. In good time you will be taken. But not on the street. Inside.

PHILIA. You will tell me when he comes?

PSEUDOLUS. I shall have him knock. On the door. Three times.

PHILIA. That's two and one more?

PSEUDOLUS. Correct. Three times. Now, in, in, in.

PHILIA *exits into* SENEX's *house.*

HERO (*despondently*). Pseudolus, what is going to happen?

PSEUDOLUS (*confidently*). She will go with you.

HYSTERIUM *enters from* SENEX's *house.*

HYSTERIUM. Hero, I am off to market. While you are alone with the girl, remember who you are.

HERO *exits into* SENEX's *house.*

I have yet to begin my daily chores.

PSEUDOLUS. Hysterium, before you go. Just one more favour.

HYSTERIUM. What is it?

PSEUDOLUS. May I borrow your book of potions?

HYSTERIUM. Oh, no, no, no! That stays right here . . . (*Pats his back pocket.*) Where it belongs. (*Calls off.*) You there, bird seller! What do you have in the way of a plump peahen?

As he exits, PSEUDOLUS *deftly lifts potion book from* HYSTERIUM's *back pocket, addresses audience.*

PSEUDOLUS. His book of potions! And my pass to freedom! What I need is his sleeping potion. With a drop or two of that, the breath stops short, the eyes slam shut, the body hangs limp. I shall mix a few drops in a beaker of wine and give it to the girl to drink. I show Lycus that she has died of the plague and tell Hero to dispose of the body. Then they to the boat, I to the hills – (*Points to audience.*) – and you to your homes. (*Looks through pages, then to audience.*) I just remembered something frightening. I cannot read! (*Calls.*) Hero! Come out here.

HERO *enters from* SENEX's *house.*

Call these pages off to me.

HERO. Not now?!

PSEUDOLUS. Yes, now! Read!

HERO (*reading as he turns pages*). 'Fever Potion' . . . 'Headache Potion' . . . 'Passion Potion' . . . 'Sleeping Potion' . . .

PSEUDOLUS. That's it! The formula. What do we need? The ingredients?

HERO. 'The eye of an eel.'

PSEUDOLUS. That we have.

HERO. 'The heart of a snail.'

PSEUDOLUS. That we have.

HERO. 'A cup of mare's sweat.'

PSEUDOLUS. Mare's sweat? That we have not.

HERO. Why are you preparing this?

PSEUDOLUS. I intend to give it to the girl. Asleep, she will go with you.

HERO. She will?

PSEUDOLUS (*worried*). Mare's sweat . . .

HERO. Where will you find it?

PSEUDOLUS. Leave that to me. *You* go to the harbour! Give the boatman your twenty minae and tell him that you sail with him this day! *I* shall prepare the potion!

HERO. This is exciting!

PSEUDOLUS. Isn't it! Go!

HERO *exits.*

Mare's sweat! Where am I going to find mare's sweat on a balmy day like this?

PSEUDOLUS *exits, as* SENEX *enters with* DOMINA'*s bust, calling.*

SENEX. Pseudolus! Pseudolus! . . . He could have taken this to the stonecutter for me. (*To audience.*) I dropped it, and now the nose has to be re-sharpened. Hysterium will take it for me.

Goes to his house, kicks door three times. A pause, then PHILIA *enters from house, arms outstretched.*

PHILIA. Take me!

SENEX *looks around.*

Take me!

SENEX. What did you say?

PHILIA. Take me!

SENEX. One moment.

Puts statue on stoop, starts for PHILIA, *returns to statue, and turns its face away from* PHILIA.

PHILIA. Here on the street if you like! My body is yours. Say it. Say it!

SENEX (*looks around, then quickly*). Your body is mine.

PHILIA. Then take me! (*Throws herself at him.*) Is this not what you want?

SENEX. It does cross my mind now and then.

PHILIA. You must know one thing.

SENEX. What is that?

PHILIA. Though you have my body, you shall never have my heart.

SENEX. Well, you can't have everything. (*Looks heavenward.*) A thousand thanks, whichever one of you did this.

She seizes him. They hold their embrace as PSEUDOLUS *enters, carrying a vial. Not seeing* SENEX *and* PHILIA, *he addresses audience.*

PSEUDOLUS. Would you believe it? There was a mare sweating not two streets from here.

Holds up vial, turns, sees embrace. SENEX*'s face is hidden from him.* PSEUDOLUS *turns to audience.*

Gets to look more like his father every day!

PHILIA (*still in* SENEX*'s arms*). Pseudolus, he is here.

PSEUDOLUS. No!

SENEX *looks from* PHILIA *to* PSEUDOLUS, *then back to* PHILIA.

SENEX. Remember where we stopped.

Slips out from under her, goes to PSEUDOLUS.

PSEUDOLUS. Sir, you're back.

SENEX (*holding his spine*). She almost broke it.

PSEUDOLUS. You've returned!

SENEX. Yes!

PSEUDOLUS. Unexpectedly!

SENEX. Apparently! Who is she?

PHILIA. I shall wait your bidding.

SENEX. Yes, dear.

PHILIA. Ever your servant. (*Bows, exits into* SENEX*'s house.*)

SENEX (*sighs*). Ever my servant.

PSEUDOLUS (*quickly*). Yes, sir. Your servant. Your new maid. We needed someone to help.

SENEX. A new maid. She seems very loyal.

PSEUDOLUS. And very efficient and very courteous and very thoughtful.

SENEX. Maids like me. I'm neat. I like maids. *They're* neat. Something no household should be without.

Sings, PSEUDOLUS *all the while encouraging him.*

Everybody ought to have a maid.
Everybody ought to have a working girl,
Everybody ought to have a lurking girl
To putter around the house.

Everybody ought to have a maid.
Everybody ought to have a menial,
Consistently congenial
And quieter than a mouse.

Oh! Oh! Wouldn't she be delicious,
Tidying up the dishes,
Neat as a pin?
Oh! Oh! Wouldn't she be delightful,
Sweeping out, sleeping in?

Everybody ought to have a maid!
Someone whom you hire when you're short of help
To offer you the sort of help
You never get from a spouse!
Fluttering up the stairway,
Shuttering up the windows,
Cluttering up the bedroom,
Buttering up the master,
Puttering all around
The house!

PSEUDOLUS *pantomimes a maid.*

Oh! Oh! Wouldn't she be delicious,
Tidying up the dishes,
Neat as a pin?
Oh! Oh! Wouldn't she be delightful,
Sweeping out, sleeping in?

Everybody ought to have a maid!
Someone who, when fetching you your slipper, will
Be winsome as a whippoorwill
And graceful as a grouse!
Skittering down the hallway,
Flittering through the parlour,
Tittering in the pantry,
Littering up the bedroom,
Twittering all around
The house!

HYSTERIUM *enters, reacts at the sight of* SENEX.
PSEUDOLUS *whispers to him.*

HYSTERIUM. A maid?

PSEUDOLUS. A maid.

SENEX. A maid.

ALL. A maid!
Everybody ought to have a maid.
Everybody ought to have a serving girl,
A loyal and unswerving girl
Who's quieter than a mouse.

Oh! Oh!
Think of her at the dustbin,
'Specially when she's just been
Traipsing about.
Oh! Oh!
Wouldn't she be delightful?

HYSTERIUM.
Living in . . .

SENEX.
Giving out!

ALL.
Everybody ought to have a maid,
Daintily collecting bits of paper 'n' strings,
Appealing in her apron strings,
Beguiling in her blouse!

HYSTERIUM.
Pattering through the attic,

SENEX.
Chattering in the cellar,

PSEUDOLUS.
Clattering in the kitchen,

SENEX.
Flattering in the bedroom,

ALL.
Puttering all around the house,
The house,
The house!

LYCUS *enters.* HYSTERIUM *whispers to him.*

LYCUS. A maid?

HYSTERIUM. A maid.

PSEUDOLUS. A maid.

SENEX. A maid!

ALL.
Everybody ought to have a maid,
Someone who's efficient and reliable,
Obedient and pliable
And quieter than a mouse.

Oh! Oh! Wouldn't she be so nimble,
Fiddling with her thimble,
Mending a gown?
Oh! Oh! Wouldn't she be delightful?

LYCUS.
Cleaning up . . .

SENEX.
Leaning down!

ALL.
Everybody ought to have a maid!
Someone who'll be busy as a bumblebee
And, even if you grumble, be
As graceful as a grouse!

LYCUS.
Wriggling in the anteroom,

HYSTERIUM.
Jiggling in the living-room,

PSEUDOLUS.
Giggling in the dining-room,

SENEX.
Wiggling in the other rooms,

ALL.
Puttering all around
The house!
The house!
The house!

LYCUS *exits into his house.*

SENEX. I know how busy both of you are. Therefore, it is for *me* to instruct her in the niceties of housework. (*Starting for his house.*) We shall start in my room.

HYSTERIUM. Sir!

PSEUDOLUS. Sir, your son is in there!

SENEX. Oh! (*Thinks a moment, then:*) Before my friend and neighbour, Erronius, went abroad in search of his children stolen in infancy by pirates, he asked me to look into his house from time to time. (*Goes to* ERRONIUS*'s house, takes key from ledge and opens door.*) This seems as good a time as any. I shall have a chat with the girl in here. Send her to me.

PSEUDOLUS. Sir.

SENEX. Yes?

PSEUDOLUS. Only my great devotion to you allows me to speak so frankly.

Unseen by SENEX, PSEUDOLUS *sprinkles contents of vial on him.*

You trudged along the road quite some way, and I fear that the great physical exertion . . . (*Sniffs.*)

SENEX (*sniffing*). Is that me?!

PSEUDOLUS. Yes, sir.

SENEX. My heavens, I smell like an overheated horse! I shall have to bathe.

PSEUDOLUS. At least!

SENEX *exits into* ERRONIUS*'s house.*

HYSTERIUM. Why did I ever let her in the house? I should never have listened to you!

PSEUDOLUS. Everything is going to be fine, pussycat. (*Hands him potion book.*)

HYSTERIUM. Oh, you! You just see that she gets out of that house.

PSEUDOLUS (*picking up statue*). And you just see that he *stays* in *that* house. Keep calm! (*Exits into* SENEX*'s house.*)

HYSTERIUM. Calm? Calm? Mustn't be excited. Calm. Calm.

Sings excitedly.

I'm calm, I'm calm,
I'm perfectly calm,
I'm utterly under control.
I haven't a worry –
Where others would hurry,
I stroll.

He runs frantically around the stage.

I'm calm, I'm cool,
A gibbering fool
Is something I never become!
When thunder is rumbling
And others are crumbling,
I hum.

He tries to hum; it becomes a stifled scream.

I must think calm, comforting things:
Butterfly wings,
Emerald rings.
Or a murmuring brook,
Murmuring, murmuring, murmuring . . .
Look:

Steadying his hands, seemingly calm.

I'm calm, I'm calm,
I haven't a qualm,
I'm utterly under control.
Let nothing confuse me
Or faze me –

Yawns.

Excuse me –

I'm calm,
Oh, so calm,
Oh, so . . .

SENEX (*calls from inside* ERRONIUS*'s house*). Hysterium!

HYSTERIUM *runs into* SENEX*'s house*. PROTEANS,
dressed as SAILORS, *enter with bags, drop them, as*
ERRONIUS *enters behind them.*

ERRONIUS. Bring up the baggage. Fetch the rest from the harbour.

SAILORS *exit.*

Ah, home at last! After years of searching for my long-lost children.

HYSTERIUM *enters from* SENEX*'s house, carrying plucked chicken, reacts in horror.*

How good it is to see this street once more. These tired old eyes fill with tears at the sight of the little they see. (*Bumps into* HYSTERIUM.) Pardon me, young woman, I was just . . . that is . . . I mean to say . . . Ah, lovely baby. (*Pats chicken.*) About the age of my children when they were stolen by pirates. (*Going to his house.*) Well, at least I have the comfort of my lonely house.

HYSTERIUM *rushes to door of* ERRONIUS*'s house.*

HYSTERIUM. Sir!

ERRONIUS. And who are you?

HYSTERIUM. Hysterium, sir, servant to Senex.

ERRONIUS (*to pillar*). Yes, of course. I should have known you anywhere.

SENEX *is heard singing from inside house a bit of 'Everybody Ought to Have a Maid'.*

What was that?

HYSTERIUM. I didn't hear anything.

SENEX *sings a bit more.*

I didn't hear that either.

ERRONIUS. You did not hear that eerie sound?

HYSTERIUM. Eerie?

ERRONIUS. Eerie, as if haunted.

HYSTERIUM (*to himself*). Eerie, as if haunted? (*To* ERRONIUS.) Sir, what I am about to tell you is eerie . . . Your house is . . . is haunted.

ERRONIUS. Haunted?

HYSTERIUM. As haunted as the day is long!

PSEUDOLUS *enters, stirring the potion, listens.*

ERRONIUS. Impossible! My house haunted, you say? Strange.

HYSTERIUM. But true. Perhaps you ought to stay with relatives . . . distant relatives.

ERRONIUS. Yes! No! Fetch me a soothsayer.

HYSTERIUM. A soothsayer?

ERRONIUS. Yes, I must have him search my house immediately.

PSEUDOLUS *puts cloth over his head, runs to* ERRONIUS, *chants ghoulishly.*

PSEUDOLUS. You are in need of a soothsayer?

ERRONIUS. How did you know?

PSEUDOLUS. I'd be a fine soothsayer if I didn't!

ERRONIUS. There is a spirit in my . . .

PSEUDOLUS. Silence! I am about to say the sooth! Wait! (*Chants incoherently.*) I see it. I see everything.

HYSTERIUM *steps behind* ERRONIUS, *pantomimes distance.*

You have been abroad.

ERRONIUS. Yes, yes.

PSEUDOLUS. For . . .

Looks at HYSTERIUM, *who flashes his ten fingers twice.*

. . . twenty years!

ERRONIUS *nods vigorously.* HYSTERIUM *shades his eyes with one hand.*

You have been searching . . . for . . .

HYSTERIUM *cradles his arms, rocks them.*

A child!

HYSTERIUM *holds up two fingers.*

Two children!

ERRONIUS. Yes, yes!

HYSTERIUM *flexes his muscles.*

PSEUDOLUS. A fine, big boy.

ERRONIUS. Yes.

PSEUDOLUS. And . . .

HYSTERIUM *places hand on his hip, pantomimes a girl.*

A strange, little boy.

HYSTERIUM *shakes his head no.*

A girl! A girl! A boy and a girl!

ERRONIUS. Yes! Can you find them for me?

PSEUDOLUS. Certainly. I can find them for you.

ERRONIUS (*takes ring from his finger, gives it to
PSEUDOLUS*). Each wears a ring on which is engraven a
gaggle of geese.

PSEUDOLUS. A gaggle of what?

ERRONIUS. A gaggle of geese. Look! (*Points to ring.*) There
are only two others like it in the world. And my children
wear them.

PSEUDOLUS. How many geese in a gaggle?

ERRONIUS. At least seven.

PSEUDOLUS. Seven? Then before I say the sooth again you
must walk seven times around the seven hills of Rome.

ERRONIUS. Seven times?

HYSTERIUM. Slowly.

ERRONIUS. Seven times around the seven hills?

SAILORS *enter with more baggage.*

Take it all back to the harbour! (*Proudly.*) *My* house is
haunted.

SAILORS *exit with baggage.* SENEX *is heard singing
again.* PSEUDOLUS *joins in, eerily.*

And the spirit?

PSEUDOLUS. It shall be gone by the time you have done my bidding.

ERRONIUS. Thank you.

PSEUDOLUS. To the hills!

ERRONIUS. To the hills!

Starts for the footlights, PSEUDOLUS *and* HYSTERIUM *stop him, head him toward the wings.*

HYSTERIUM. This is the way, sir!

ERRONIUS. Thank you, young woman! (*Exits.*)

PSEUDOLUS (*calls*). Sir, you forgot your gaggle!

Puts ring on his own finger. SENEX *enters from* ERRONIUS*'s house.*

SENEX. Hysterium!

HYSTERIUM (*jumping*). Sir!

SENEX. Prepare my bath!

HYSTERIUM. Yes, sir! (*Runs into* ERRONIUS*'s house.*)

SENEX. Ah, Pseudolus, that little maid. Do you know what her first words were to me? She said 'Take me.'

PSEUDOLUS (*picking up potion bowl*). And you shall, sir.

SENEX. . . . I'll try.

PSEUDOLUS (*exiting into* SENEX*'s house*). Yes, sir.

SENEX (*starting into* ERRONIUS*'s house*). Remember, Hysterium. Not too hot and not too cold.

HERO *runs on, calling.*

HERO. Philia! Philia!

SENEX (*stops in doorway, turns*). Son!

HERO. Father! Where's mother?

SENEX (*frightened, turns*). Where?! (*Realises.*) Oh. I – I have returned without her. Pressing business.

PHILIA *appears on balcony of* SENEX*'s house.*

(*Aside to* HERO.) Lovely new maid.

HERO. New maid?

SENEX. Pseudolus told me about it.

HERO. Oh.

SENEX (*to* PHILIA). Presently, my dear.

> PHILIA *exits into house, waving.* SENEX *turns to audience, sings.*

> Why did he look at her that way?

HERO (*sings, to audience*).
> Why did he look at her that way?

BOTH.
> Must be my imagination . . .

SENEX.
> She's a lovely blooming flower,
> He's just a sprout – impossible!

HERO.
> She's a lovely blooming flower,
> He's all worn out – impossible!

SENEX.
> Just a fledgling in the nest . . .

HERO.
> Just a man who needs a rest . . .

SENEX.
> He's a beamish boy at best . . .

HERO.
> Poor old fellow . . .

SENEX.
> He's a child and love's a test
> He's too young to pass – impassable!

HERO.
> He has asthma, gout, a wife,
> Lumbago and gas – irascible!

SENEX.
> Romping in the nursery . . .

HERO.
> He looks tired . . .

SENEX (*to* HERO, *warmly*).
  Son, sit on your father's knee.

HERO (*to* SENEX, *warmly*).
  Father, you can lean on me.

BOTH (*to audience*).
  Him?
  Impossible!

HERO.
  But why did she wave at him that way?

SENEX.
  Why did she wave at him that way?

 BOTH.
  Could there be an explanation?

HERO.
  Women often want a father,
  She may want mine – it's possible!

SENEX.
  He's a handsome lad of twenty,
  I'm thirty-nine – it's possible!

HERO.
  Older men know so much more . . .

SENEX.
  In a way, I'm forty-four . . .

HERO.
  Next to him, I'll seem a bore . . .

SENEX.
  All right, fifty!

HERO.
  Then again, he *is* my father,
  I ought to trust – impossible!

SENEX.
  Then again, with love at my age,
  Sometimes it's just – impossible!

HERO.
  With a girl, I'm ill-at-ease . . .

SENEX.
I don't feel well . . .

HERO (*to* SENEX, *helplessly*).
Sir, about those birds and bees . . .

SENEX (*to* HERO, *helplessly*).
Son, a glass of water, please . . .

BOTH (*to audience*).
The situation's fraught,
Fraughter than I thought,
With horrible,
Impossible
Possibilities!

SENEX (*calling to his house*). Pseudolus! (*To* HERO.) Son, it grieves me to see a boy your age moping about the house.

PSEUDOLUS *enters, stirring potion.*

Pseudolus, I want you to take Hero to the baths.

HERO. Sir!

PSEUDOLUS. Very good, sir. Allow me to finish a brew master Hero asked me to prepare. (*To* HERO.) Master, I shall meet you in front of the baths of Aqua Salina. You know where it is? Next to the harbour. And I shall have a surprise for you.

HERO. Oh, yes. Yes, of course. Farewell, father. Farewell, Pseudolus. (*Exits.*)

SENEX. Well, he to his bath and I to mine.

HYSTERIUM *enters from* ERRONIUS*'s house, wiping hands on tunic.*

HYSTERIUM. Just the way you like it, sir.

SENEX. One thing more, Hysterium.

HYSTERIUM. Yes, sir?

SENEX. I shall need a complete change of garb. Let me see . . . my tunic with the tassels!

HYSTERIUM. Sir, it needs taking in.

SENEX. Well, take it in and bring it out!

Exits into ERRONIUS's *house.* HYSTERIUM *exits into*
SENEX's *house singing a bit of 'I'm Calm.'* LYCUS *enters
from his house.*

LYCUS. Pseudolus! The girl! I want to know the worst. How
is she?

PSEUDOLUS. She is very low.

LYCUS. Still smiling?

PSEUDOLUS. Laughing!

LYCUS *reacts in horror.*

There is one hope! I have prepared a plague potion. If it is
not too late, we may yet save her life.

LYCUS. Give it to her!

PSEUDOLUS. Yes!

PSEUDOLUS *starts for* SENEX's *house as fanfare is heard
and* PROTEAN, *dressed as* SOLDIER, *enters, carrying
spear.*

SOLDIER. Ho, there!

They turn, stare at him with horror.

I seek the house of Marcus Lycus.

LYCUS (*stammering superbly*). Who heeks the souse of
Mycus Leecus?

PSEUDOLUS (*a hand on* LYCUS's *shoulder*). Hold, sir.

LYCUS. But he . . . who . . .

PSEUDOLUS. You're not holding. (*To* SOLDIER, *enunciating
grotesquely.*) Who is he who seeks the house of Marcus
Lycus?

SOLDIER. A foot soldier of Captain Miles Gloriosus!

Executes an elaborate salute. Fanfare.

PSEUDOLUS. Smartly done!

SOLDIER. My captain has dispatched me to inform you that
he is but half a league away. Prepare to greet him!

Salutes, exits. Fanfare.

PSEUDOLUS. Half a league!

LYCUS. We have only moments!

PSEUDOLUS. I'll give her the potion!

LYCUS. Yes!

PSEUDOLUS. Yes! (*Starts for* SENEX*'s house.*)

LYCUS. Wait!

PSEUDOLUS (*returns to* LYCUS). What?

LYCUS. Don't leave me!

PSEUDOLUS. Why not?

LYCUS. He's coming!

PSEUDOLUS. I know he's coming!

LYCUS (*takes bowl from him*). You speak to him. *I'll* give her the potion!

PSEUDOLUS. Wait! You can't give her the potion!

LYCUS. Why not?

PSEUDOLUS. You'll catch the plague!

LYCUS (*hands him bowl quickly*). Oh, I don't want the plague!

PSEUDOLUS. I've got to give her the potion!

LYCUS. Yes!

PSEUDOLUS. Yes! (*Starts for* SENEX*'s house.*)

LYCUS. Wait!

PSEUDOLUS (*returns to* LYCUS). What?

LYCUS. She is in the house of Senex!

PSEUDOLUS. What will we do? . . . Does he know which house is your house?

LYCUS. No!

PSEUDOLUS (*points to* SENEX*'s house*). *This* is your house!

LYCUS. Will he believe it?

PSEUDOLUS. Get the girls!

LYCUS. Good!

PSEUDOLUS. I'll give her the potion!

LYCUS. And I'll get the girls!

PSEUDOLUS. Good!

LYCUS. Yes!

PSEUDOLUS. Yes! (*Starts for* SENEX's *house.*)

LYCUS. Wait!

PSEUDOLUS (*returns to* LYCUS). *What is it??!!*

LYCUS. I forgot.

PSEUDOLUS. Lycus, we must not lose our heads!

LYCUS. Yes! No!

PSEUDOLUS (*screams*). We must remain serene!

Fanfare is heard.

LYCUS. Pseudolus, *you* must speak to the captain! I have no talent for bravery.

PSEUDOLUS. You grant me permission to represent you?

LYCUS. Complete!

PSEUDOLUS. All right. Collect the courtesans and bring them out. Then you are to wait in your house.

LYCUS. Pseudolus, I am eternally grateful. I am your friend until death!

PSEUDOLUS. Go!

LYCUS. Yes!

PSEUDOLUS. Yes! (*Starts for* SENEX's *house.*)

LYCUS. Wait!

PSEUDOLUS (*stops, yells*). No!

A fanfare, and two PROTEANS, *dressed as* SOLDIERS, *enter, come to a smart halt.* LYCUS *ducks into his house.* PSEUDOLUS *puts down potion bowl.*

SECOND SOLDIER. Ho, there!

THIRD SOLDIER. We seek the house of Marcus Lycus!

PSEUDOLUS. Who seeks the mouse of Larkus Heekus?

THIRD SOLDIER. Foot soldiers of Captain Miles Gloriosus.

SECOND SOLDIER. He is but a quarter of a league away and bids you honour this. (*Hands* PSEUDOLUS *parchment.*)

PSEUDOLUS (*studies parchment*). Oh, yes, of course.

SECOND SOLDIER. You know what this is?

PSEUDOLUS. Of course I know what this is. This is writing.

THIRD SOLDIER. It is your contract with the captain.

PSEUDOLUS. And a pretty piece of work. What is this word here? (*Points to spot on parchment.*)

THIRD SOLDIER. That is 'Lycus'.

PSEUDOLUS. Oh, yes. Then you realise whom you are speaking to.

SECOND SOLDIER. Yes, sir.

THIRD SOLDIER. And do you see what it says there? (*Points to another spot.*)

PSEUDOLUS. It says . . . words. And I intend to stand behind those words, or my name is not Marcus Lycus!

HYSTERIUM *enters.*

HYSTERIUM. Pseudolus!

PSEUDOLUS (*without missing a beat*). Or my name is not Pseudolus Marcus Lycus! A moment. I must have a word with my eunuch. (*Taking* HYSTERIUM *aside.*) Come here, eunuch!

HYSTERIUM. How dare you call me that?

PSEUDOLUS. You know it's not true, and I know it's not true, so what do we care what they think?

HYSTERIUM. Those soldiers, have they come for the girl? I'll go right in and get her.

PSEUDOLUS. They have not come for the girl. They have come for me.

HYSTERIUM. What?

PSEUDOLUS. Hysterium, I have never told you this, but years ago I deserted from the army.

HYSTERIUM. No!

PSEUDOLUS. Sh! I was very young. I wanted to be an archer. Instead, they made me a slinger. Then, one day, at the height of battle, I lost my head. I arched when I should have slung. I had to flee.

HYSTERIUM. And now they have found you. Oh, Pseudolus!

PSEUDOLUS. Sh! They are looking for Pseudolus. I told them I am Lycus.

HYSTERIUM. And Lycus you are! Rely on me!

PSEUDOLUS. I must. (*Picks up potion bowl.*) Hysterium, more bad news!

HYSTERIUM. I hope it's good.

PSEUDOLUS. It's terrible! The girl refuses to go with her captain. That is why I have prepared your sleeping potion. You are to give her a drop or two in a beaker of wine, and upon hearing me say 'Present the bride', carry her out in your arms!

HYSTERIUM. Trust me, Pseu – (*Catches himself, then loudly.*) Trust me, Lycus!

Takes bowl from PSEUDOLUS, *speaking for* SOLDIERS' *benefit.*

I go, Lycus. Farewell, Lycus! (*Exits into* SENEX's *house.*)

PSEUDOLUS (*to* SOLDIERS). Bid your captain come! His bride awaits him!

SOLDIERS *execute fancy salute, run off.* PSEUDOLUS *calls out.*

Lycus! The girls! Quickly!

LYCUS (*opening his door*). Yes! (*Calls into house.*) Eunuchs! The girls! Quickly! (*To* PSEUDOLUS.) We shall pose them informally!

PSEUDOLUS. Give the place a friendly look.

EUNUCHS *herd* COURTESANS *out of house.*

EUNUCH. Hurry, there! Hurry! Hurry!

GYMNASIA. Don't you lower your voice to me!

LYCUS. You are to do exactly as Pseudolus bids. He will represent me.

PSEUDOLUS (*points to* SENEX*'s house*). All you girls over here! Now, you eunuchs . . .

Indicates manly pose he wants them to assume. EUNUCHS *squeal with delight.*

Lycus, do we really need these eunuchs?

LYCUS (*to* EUNUCHS). Into the house.

EUNUCHS (*chirping*). Into the house! Into the house!

EUNUCHS *exit into* LYCUS*'s house.* PSEUDOLUS *arranges* COURTESANS.

PSEUDOLUS (*to* PANACEA). You there. (*To* TINTINABULA *and* VIBRATA.) You there. (*To* GEMINAE.) You there. (*To* GYMNASIA.) You there . . . Oh, there's so much of you there!

He leans on her bosom, as ERRONIUS *enters.*

ERRONIUS (*to audience*). First time around!

All watch as he crosses stage, exits.

PSEUDOLUS (*to* COURTESANS). Now, may I have your attention? You are about to meet a great captain. Remember who you are and what you stand for. Now, will you all please strike . . . vocational attitudes?

COURTESANS *strike poses.*

Perfect! I would like a mosaic of this scene. An entire wall made up of . . .

Fanfare is heard.

LYCUS. The captain! Pseudolus, again my heartfelt . . .

PSEUDOLUS. In! In!

LYCUS *exits into his house. A second fanfare is heard.*

MILES (*offstage*). Stand aside, everyone! I take large steps!

Enters with SOLDIERS, *counting off, music under.*

SOLDIERS.
One, two, one, two . . .

MILES.

We not only fought but we won, too!

SOLDIERS.

One, two, one, two . . .
Left, right, left, right . . .

MILES.

There's none of the enemy left, right?

SOLDIERS. Right! Left! . . . uh . . . Ri – uh – left!

Utter confusion.

MILES. Halt!

PSEUDOLUS (*saluting*). Hail, Miles Gloriosus.

MILES. You are?

PSEUDOLUS. Marcus Lycus, sir. I am dazzled by your
presence.

MILES. Everyone is.

PSEUDOLUS (*indicating* SENEX*'s house*). Welcome to my
house, great captain. Your bride awaits you.

MILES. My bride!

Sings.

My bride! My bride!
I've come to claim my bride,
Come tenderly to crush her against my side!
Let haste be made,
I cannot be delayed!
There are lands to conquer,
Cities to loot,
And peoples to degrade!

SOLDIERS.

Look at those arms!
Look at that chest!
Look at them!

MILES.

Not to mention the rest!
Even I am impressed.

My bride! My bride!
Come bring to me my bride!

My lust for her no longer can be denied!
Convey the news,
I have no time to lose!
There are towns to plunder,
Temples to burn
And women to abuse!

SOLDIERS.
Look at that foot!
Look at that heel!
Mark the magnificent muscles of steel!

MILES.
I am my ideal!

I, Miles Gloriosus,
I, slaughterer of thousands,
I, oppressor of the meek,
Subduer of the weak,
Degrader of the Greek,
Destroyer of the Turk,
Must hurry back to work!

MILES.	COURTESANS.	SOLDIERS.
I, Miles Gloriosus,	Him, Miles Gloriosus,	A man among men!
I, paragon of virtues,	Him, paragon of virtues,	With sword and
		with pen!

MILES.	ALL.
I, in war the most admired,	Himmm!
In wit the most inspired,	Himmm!
In love the most desired,	Himmm!
In dress the best displayed,	
I am a parade!	

SOLDIERS.
Look at those eyes,
Cunning and keen!
Look at the size of those thighs,
Like a mighty machine!

PSEUDOLUS.
Those are the mightiest thighs that I ever have theen!
I mean . . .

MILES.
>My bride! My bride!
>Inform my lucky bride:
>The fabled arms of Miles are open wide!
>Make haste! Make haste!
>I have no time to waste!
>There are shrines I should be sacking,
>Ribs I should be cracking,
>Eyes to gouge and booty to divide!
>Bring me my bride!

SOLDIERS.
>Bring him his bride!

ALL.
>Bring him his bride!

>*PSEUDOLUS goes to SENEX's house.*

PSEUDOLUS. Present the bride!

>*Fanfare.*

>Pay homage all! Here, in one being is Juno, Diana and Venus.

>*All kneel.*

>Present the bride!

>*Fanfare.* PSEUDOLUS *bows.* HYSTERIUM *enters.*

>(*To* MILES.) A short delay, sir! (*Pulls* HYSTERIUM *aside.*) What happened?

HYSTERIUM. I'll tell you what happened! Nothing! She won't drink!

PSEUDOLUS. What?

HYSTERIUM. She says on Crete her religion forbids it.

PSEUDOLUS. He had to fall in love with a religious Cretan! *I'll* get her to drink! Captain, forgive the girl. She primps and preens. She wants to be worthy of so great a warrior.

>*Exits into* SENEX's house with HYSTERIUM.

MILES. Understandable. I *am* a legend in my own time.

>*Laughs.* SOLDIERS *join in.*

>Men! Close ranks! Stand tall!

PSEUDOLUS *enters from* SENEX*'s house.*

Lycus!

LYCUS *peeks out of upper window of his house, listens.*

Where is my bride?

PSEUDOLUS. Did she not come through this door?

MILES. No! What are you saying, man?

PSEUDOLUS. The virgin has escaped!

MILES. Oh, no! The beautiful bride I bargained for!

PSEUDOLUS. Vanished!

MILES. This is monstrous!

PSEUDOLUS. It certainly is. But look at it this way. Since I cannot deliver her to you, you do not have to pay me the five hundred minae.

MILES. I *paid* you the five hundred minae!

PSEUDOLUS *reacts.*

Through my agents. Has the money escaped as well?

PSEUDOLUS. There has been a little mistake. (*Laughs weakly.*) I was only joking. Lycus will pay you.

LYCUS *groans, disappears from window.*

MILES. What?

PSEUDOLUS. I was helping out a friend. Allow me, great captain.

He goes to LYCUS*'s house, pulls* LYCUS *out.*

Come out here! (*To* MILES.) Here is your man! (*To* LYCUS.) Tell him! Tell him who I am!

HYSTERIUM *enters.*

LYCUS. Everyone knows who you are, *Lycus.*

HYSTERIUM. Of course. He is Marcus Lycus.

PSEUDOLUS. No! No! *He* is Lycus. *This* is his house!

LYCUS (*to* MILES). Look within, sir. You will find none here but hooded men. We are a holy order. An ancient brotherhood of lepers.

MILES *backs away.*

Unclean! Unclean! And bless you, Lycus! (*He backs offstage.*)

MILES. What now, Lycus?

PSEUDOLUS. What?

MILES. I shall tell you what! With axe and pike, my soldiers shall raze this house to the ground!

HYSTERIUM (*fainting*). Our beautiful house!

MILES. And you, you shall receive the maximum punishment – death!

COURTESANS *scream.*

PSEUDOLUS. Please, sir, please! May I be allowed a word?

MILES. A word?

PSEUDOLUS. One word.

MILES. It had better be a good one.

PSEUDOLUS. Oh, it is, sir!

MILES. What is it?

PSEUDOLUS (*to audience*). Intermission!

Curtain.

ACT TWO

The scene is the same as Act One, but now PROLOGUS *is played by* SENEX *rather than by* PSEUDOLUS. *As characters enter, they assume the positions in which we last saw them at the end of Act One.*

PROLOGUS. Welcome again, playgoers. You are about to witness the second half of our play.

Signals orchestra, which plays under following.

Permit me to remind you where we were when last you saw us. The virgin . . .

PHILIA *enters.*

. . . was waiting . . . that's what they do best . . . waiting here in the house for her captain to claim her. She has refused to drink the potion on religious grounds.

PHILIA *exits into* SENEX's *house.*

Lycus . . .

LYCUS *enters.*

. . . skulks about the city, searching for Philia.

LYCUS *exits.*

Hero . . .

HERO *enters.*

. . . is at the baths where he sits and soaks.

HERO *exits.*

His mother . . .

DOMINA *enters, exits.*

. . . is on the way to the country to visit *her* mother. A hundred and four years old, and not one organ in working condition. The courtesans . . .

COURTESANS *enter.*

. . . Miles Gloriosus and his mighty warriors . . .

MILES, SOLDIERS *enter.*

. . . Hysterium and Pseudolus are here.

HYSTERIUM, PSEUDOLUS *enter.*

And I, Senex, await the maid in my neighbour's house, hopefully about to sow my last oat, if memory serves. Let the play continue! (*Exits into* ERRONIUS*'s house.*)

PSEUDOLUS (*to* MILES). Sir! I . . .

MILES (*to* SOLDIERS). Gag him!

SOLDIER *grabs* PSEUDOLUS *from behind, clamps hand over his mouth.*

And now I rid Rome of a rascal!

He pulls his sword back, and as he is about to send it into PSEUDOLUS *at belly level,* PSEUDOLUS *whirls around, and the sword jabs* SOLDIER *in the rear.* SOLDIER *releases* PSEUDOLUS, *jumps away rubbing sore spot.* MILES *advances on* PSEUDOLUS.

You . . .

PSEUDOLUS. Sir!

MILES *stalks him, as* PSEUDOLUS *speaks glibly.*

The girl must be near at hand. If you kill me you deprive yourself of seeing a face so fair, a heart so pure, a body so undulating . . .

MILES *lowers his sword.* PSEUDOLUS, *sensing success, presses on.*

She is magnificence personified! If you had been born a woman, you would have been she!

MILES. As magnificent as that?

PSEUDOLUS. Yes, sir. Spare me! I am sure she can be found.

MILES. You are?

PSEUDOLUS. Yes, sir. I shall give you a list of ten or twenty places you might look for her.

MILES. *You* shall look for her!

PSEUDOLUS. Me? With this bad leg?

Limps horribly. MILES *grabs him.*

MILES. With that bad leg!

PSEUDOLUS. Yes, it will do it good. And where may I deliver the girl? I mean, where will you be?

MILES (*points to* SENEX's *house*). Waiting here in your house.

HYSTERIUM. No!

MILES. No?!

HYSTERIUM. I meant 'yes', it just came out 'no'.

MILES (*to* PSEUDOLUS). And to assure your return . . . Men! You are to go with him.

PSEUDOLUS. Sir, before I go, a word with my eunuch.

MILES. Be brief.

PSEUDOLUS. Yes, sir. Come here, eunuch. (*Pulls* HYSTERIUM *aside.*) Hysterium, this is what you must do. Hide the girl, up on the roof.

HYSTERIUM. Why?

They are both stumped, then PSEUDOLUS *has the answer:*

PSEUDOLUS. Why not? Go.

MILES (*to* SOLDIERS). He is not to stray from your sight.

HYSTERIUM *exits into* SENEX's *house.*

PSEUDOLUS (*to* MILES). My eunuch is making sure the house is fit to receive so illustrious a visitor.

MILES. I have been put off enough for one day!

Turns to enter house, stops, as ERRONIUS *enters.*

ERRONIUS. The second time around!

Exits, all watch him.

MILES. Lycus!

PSEUDOLUS. Yes, sir! (*Calls.*) Ready?

HYSTERIUM (*from inside* SENEX's *house*). Ready!

PSEUDOLUS. All is ready, sir. There is food and drink within. And the girls will sing and dance for you.

COURTESANS *exit into* SENEX*'s house.*

MILES. You have but one hour. Men, you are to hound his every step.

Exits into SENEX*'s house.* PSEUDOLUS *circles stage, followed by* SOLDIERS, *they exit.* SENEX *appears in window of* ERRONIUS*'s house.*

SENEX. Hysterium!

HYSTERIUM *re-enters.*

HYSTERIUM. Yes, sir!

SENEX. Tell the little maid I am almost ready.

HYSTERIUM. Sir, I must say this to you. Abandon this mad adventure! Think of your wife on the way to the country!

SENEX. *That,* Hysterium, is the country's problem.

HYSTERIUM. Yes, sir.

SENEX. Hysterium, one thing more. You know that potion you prepare that so fills one with passion, one can almost perform miracles?

HYSTERIUM. Yes, sir. We have some left over from your last anniversary.

SENEX. Bring it to me now, slave-in-chief. (*Exits into house.*)

HYSTERIUM. Slave-in-chief! I wonder how many slaves-in-chief have a master in the tub, a house full of courtesans, and a virgin on the roof.

Exits into SENEX*'s house, as* PSEUDOLUS *enters, closely followed by* SOLDIERS. *He does several intricate manoeuvres which the* SOLDIERS *carefully follow. The manoeuvres become more elaborate.* PANACEA *enters from* SENEX*'s house, and* SOLDIERS *follow her off.*

PSEUDOLUS (*to audience*). Just one hour. Pretending she was dead was the perfect plan. If only Philia had taken one sip . . . It still is the perfect plan, if I can only find a body. A body. (*An inspiration.*) Gusto! Gusto, the bodysnatcher! He owes me a favour!

He runs off, not seeing DOMINA, *who enters, addresses audience.*

DOMINA. Since sending my husband back to Rome, I have been haunted by the premonition that he is up to something low. (*Calls.*) Hysterium!

HYSTERIUM (*entering from* SENEX'S *house with cup*). Coming master . . . mistress! You're home!

DOMINA. And parched with thirst, ever-thoughtful Hysterium.

She reaches for cup, he pulls it away.

HYSTERIUM. No! It's a potion!

DOMINA. What sort of potion?

HYSTERIUM. To make you thirsty. And you're already thirsty, so you don't need it. (*Puts cup near* ERRONIUS'S *house.*)

DOMINA. Thirst is the lesser of my problems. Hysterium, on the best of intuition, I believe my husband is fouling the nest.

HYSTERIUM (*looking nervously at* ERRONIUS'S *house*). No! Never!

DOMINA. Never? Old friend and confidant, you are talking to a woman who faces facts.

Sings.

For over thirty years,
I've cried myself to sleep,
Assailed by doubts and fears
So great the gods themselves would weep!
The moment I am gone,
I wonder where he'll go.
In all your simple honesty,
You can't begin to know . . .
Ohhhh . . .

Wailing tenderly.

I want him,
I need him,
Where is he?

Furiously.

That dirty old man is here somewhere,
Cavorting with someone young and fair,
Disporting in every shameless whim,
Just wait till I get my hands on him!

Tenderly.

I'll hold him,
Enfold him,
Where is he?

Furiously.

That dirty old man, where can he be?
Profaning our vows for all to see,
Complaining how he's misunderstood,
Abusing me (if he only would!)

Oh, love,
Sweet love,
Why hide?
You vermin, you worm, you villain!
Come face,
Embrace
Your bride!
Wherever he is, I know he's still an

Angel,
My angel!
Where is he,
That dirty old man divine?
I love him,
I love him,
That lecherous, lewd, lascivious,
Loathsome, lying, lazy,
Dirty old man of mine!

MILES (*from inside* SENEX's *house*). Why?

DOMINA. Ah, I hear him now!

MILES. Why must I always be surrounded by fawning
admirers?

DOMINA. That is not my husband's voice. Tell me, who is in
my house?

HYSTERIUM. I think it's a captain.

DOMINA. A captain?

HYSTERIUM. Yes . . . he thinks that . . . your house . . . is the . . . I hope you do not object to my offering him your hospitality.

DOMINA. Object? When I, myself, am the daughter of a Roman general? Hysterium, I must meet him.

HYSTERIUM. You wouldn't like him. He's very vulgar.

DOMINA. All soldiers are, in a grand sort of way.

MILES *appears in doorway.*

MILES. . . . interminable! (*Shouts at* HYSTERIUM.) Bring more food and drink, eunuch!

HYSTERIUM (*to* DOMINA). You see?

DOMINA. Captain, I was just coming inside to give you a proper welcome.

HYSTERIUM *winces.*

MILES (*thinking she is one of* LYCUS's *girls*). You are of this house?

DOMINA. For years and years. You know, Captain, my father was General Magnus.

MILES *reacts.*

On the last anniversary of his death, I entertained over two hundred officers.

MILES. Two hundred? By yourself?

DOMINA. Of course not. Hysterium here was a big help.

HYSTERIUM *smiles proudly, then reacts painfully.*

But now my business takes me to the Forum, but I shall return. And for the length of your stay I shall bend over backwards to please you.

MILES (*horrified*). That will not be necessary! (*Exits into* SENEX'S *house.*)

DOMINA. I do wish I could chat on with him, but I must find out why my husband was so anxious to return to Rome.

Hysterium, when next we meet I shall be in some form of disguise. If you recognise me, not a word.

Waving to MILES, *who appears in door of house.*

Until later, Captain.

MILES *moans, exits into house.* DOMINA *starts off, as* PSEUDOLUS *enters, sees her, starts polishing pillar.*

Ah, Pseudolus, busy as ever.

PSEUDOLUS. Yes, madam.

She exits. PSEUDOLUS *rushes to* HYSTERIUM.

She's back!

HYSTERIUM. Yes!

PSEUDOLUS. What has happened?

HYSTERIUM. What *hasn't* happened?

PSEUDOLUS. All right, what *hasn't* happened? She hasn't found out anything, has she?

HYSTERIUM. No!

PSEUDOLUS. Good!

HYSTERIUM. But she will, and she'll kill me!

PSEUDOLUS. No, she won't!

HYSTERIUM. No, she won't. I'll kill myself! I can do it painlessly. If she does it, it will hurt. I must do it. I have besmirched the honour of my family. My father will turn in his grave.

PSEUDOLUS. Your father is alive.

HYSTERIUM. This will kill him!

PSEUDOLUS. Are you finished? Now, listen to this. I have really shocking news.

HYSTERIUM. What?

PSEUDOLUS. You know Gusto, the bodysnatcher?

HYSTERIUM *nods.*

He died this morning.

HYSTERIUM. No! I saw him only yesterday. When is he to be buried?

PSEUDOLUS. They don't know. Someone snatched the body.

HYSTERIUM. Isn't that a sha – ?

Does a take.

Why are we crying over a dead bodysnatcher?!

PSEUDOLUS. Because he could have helped us. He could have lent us a body. (*Puts his hand on* HYSTERIUM's *shoulder.*)

HYSTERIUM. A body?

PSEUDOLUS. A body.

A gleam comes into his eye, starts running his hand over HYSTERIUM's *shoulder and chest.*

A body. Hysterium, would you like everything to be the way it was when you woke up this morning?

HYSTERIUM. In a minute!

PSEUDOLUS. That's all it will take. Come!

Pulls HYSTERIUM *to* LYCUS's *house.*

HYSTERIUM. In here?

PSEUDOLUS. In here!

HYSTERIUM. Where did you get the money?

PSEUDOLUS *pulls* HYSTERIUM *into* LYCUS's *house.* SENEX *enters from* ERRONIUS's *house, inhales deeply.*

SENEX. Mmmmmmm. (*To audience.*) Something smells divine, and it's me. I just took the most luxurious bath. The oil, the essences. Oh, spectators, I would love to pass among you so that each and everyone might get a good whiff. (*Calls.*) Philia! (*To himself.*) Mustn't shout. I have to save every bit of energy. (*Gently.*) Philia.

PHILIA *appears on roof of* SENEX's *house.*

PHILIA. Yes, master? Master?

SENEX (*looks around for her, then sees her on roof*). Ah, my dear. No need to dust up there. Come to me.

PHILIA. I am yours.

SENEX. Yes, my dear. But not on the roof. Join me in this house.

PHILIA. Yes, sir.

SENEX exits into ERRONIUS*'s house. As* PHILIA *disappears from roof,* MILES *appears on balcony of* SENEX*'s house.*

MILES. Oh, where is he? If he does not bring me my bride he shall see me at the height of my wrath.

Looks down, gets dizzy, emits a tiny scream, and staggers back into house. PHILIA *enters from* SENEX*'s house, as* HERO *runs on.*

HERO. Philia!

PHILIA. In time to say farewell.

HERO. Did not Pseudolus give you a beaker of wine?

PHILIA. My religion forbids the drinking of wine.

HERO. Oh, no!

PHILIA. Oh, yes.

HERO. Oh, Philia.

PHILIA. The captain. I must go to him.

HERO. I hate him.

PHILIA. So do I. And I have a way to make him suffer.

Sings.

Let the captain wed me and woo me,
I shall play my part!
Let him make his mad passion to me,
You will have my heart!
He can have the body he paid for,
Nothing but the body he paid for!
When he has the body he paid for,
Our revenge will start!

When I kiss him,
I'll be kissing you,
So I'll kiss him morning and night,
That'll show him!

When I hold him,
I'll be holding you,
So I'll hold him ten times as tight,
That'll show him, too!

I shall coo and tenderly stroke his hair.
Wish that you were there –
You'd enjoy it!

When it's evening
And we're in our tent for two,
I'll sit on his knee,
Get to know him
Intimately,
That'll show him
How much I really love you!

PSEUDOLUS *enters from* LYCUS*'s house.*

HERO. Pseudolus!

PSEUDOLUS. What has happened? Why are you not on the – ?

HERO. Her captain has come!

PSEUDOLUS. Where is he?

PHILIA (*points to* ERRONIUS*'s house*). In there.

PSEUDOLUS. In there . . . ? (*Realises she is referring to* SENEX.) No, no, he *was* in there. He had to go to the Senate for an unexpected ovation.

HERO. Really?

PSEUDOLUS (*shaking his head no*). Of course.

PHILIA. Does he still want me to wait on the roof?

PSEUDOLUS. Yes.

MILES (*from inside* SENEX*'s house*). Leave me alone!

PSEUDOLUS. No! Wait – uh – in the garden!

PHILIA. In the garden?

PSEUDOLUS. Yes. Behind that large clump of myrrh!

PHILIA. You will tell me when he comes?

PSEUDOLUS. Don't we always?

PHILIA. Oh, Hero, if only you could come buy me from the captain.

PSEUDOLUS. If Hero has the captain's contract, you will go with him?

PHILIA *nods yes.*

It shall be arranged. Into the garden.

HERO *and* PHILIA *exit into garden.* PSEUDOLUS *hums 'Free' as he pushes bench centre stage. He calls.*

Come out here! Come on out!

HYSTERIUM *enters from* LYCUS*'s house in virginal gown and wig.*

HYSTERIUM. You didn't tell me I'd have to be a girl!

PSEUDOLUS. A dead girl! The captain will see you, go on his way, and all will be well.

HYSTERIUM. No! It won't do!

He starts back into house. PSEUDOLUS *stops him.*

PSEUDOLUS. Please, Hysterium. We must convince the captain.

HYSTERIUM. That I am a beautiful dead girl?

PSEUDOLUS. Yes.

HYSTERIUM. He'll never believe it.

PSEUDOLUS. He will. You're delicious.

HYSTERIUM. What if he tries to kiss me?

PSEUDOLUS. He won't kiss you.

HYSTERIUM. How can he help it – if I'm so delicious?

PSEUDOLUS. Hysterium, please – just lie on the bench.

HYSTERIUM. He'll never believe I'm a girl. Look at me. Just look at me.

PSEUDOLUS. I can't take my eyes off you.

Sings.

You're lovely,
Absolutely lovely,
Who'd believe the loveliness of you?

HYSTERIUM. No!

PSEUDOLUS. Come back!

Sings.

Perfect,
Sweet and warm and winsome,
Radiant as in some dream come true.
Now
Venus will seem tame,
Helen and her thousand ships
Will have to die of shame!

HYSTERIUM *is becoming convinced;* PSEUDOLUS
presses his advantage.

You're so lovely,
Frighteningly lovely,
That the world will never seem the same!

Gently forces HYSTERIUM *to lie back on the bench, folds
his arms. Speaks.*

Now, lie there, close your eyes, and think dead thoughts.
Good!

Starts into SENEX's *house, stops, with disgust, as*
HYSTERIUM *sits up and sings.*

HYSTERIUM.
I'm lovely,
Absolutely lovely,
Who'd believe the loveliness of me?
Perfect,
Sweet and warm and winsome,
Radiant as in some dream come true.

PSEUDOLUS *forces him down on bench.*

Now . . .

Speaks.

Shouldn't I have jewellery?

PSEUDOLUS. Jewellery?

Thinks for a moment, takes ERRONIUS's *ring from his
finger, slips it on* HYSTERIUM.

HYSTERIUM. Flowers.

PSEUDOLUS. What?

HYSTERIUM. I should have flowers.

> PSEUDOLUS *gives flower to* HYSTERIUM. *Sings.*

I'm so lovely –

PSEUDOLUS.
Literally lovely –

BOTH.
That the world will never seem the same –

PSEUDOLUS.
You look lovely –

BOTH.
That the world will never seem the same!

> PSEUDOLUS *gets him down on bench once more, covers his face with the veil, and folds his arms.*

PSEUDOLUS. Fold the arms!

HYSTERIUM (*sitting up*). Any coins he puts in my eyes, I keep!

> PSEUDOLUS *pushes* HYSTERIUM *down*

FIRST SOLDIER (*offstage*). Ho, there!

> SOLDIERS *run on in pursuit of* PANACEA, *who exits into* SENEX's *house.* PSEUDOLUS *stops* SOLDIERS.

PSEUDOLUS. I have been looking everywhere for you. Here is your captain's bride. Dead!

> SOLDIERS *crowd around* HYSTERIUM.

Give her air!

They jump back.

You had best break the sad news to your captain.

> SOLDIERS *are reluctant.* FIRST SOLDIER *is pushed forward by others. He enters* SENEX's *house fearfully.* PSEUDOLUS *looks at* HYSTERIUM, *then to* SOLDIERS.

A virgin. A lot of good it did her.

MILES *enters with* FIRST SOLDIER.

MILES. Oh, grievous day. Men, support me!

SOLDIERS *hold him.*

How? How did she die?

PSEUDOLUS. Well, she just sort of rolled over and . . .

MILES. Spare me! I cannot control my tears. I must cry.

PSEUDOLUS. Go ahead, you'll feel better. Now that you have seen her, sir, I suggest you depart and torture yourself no longer. If you'll give me the contract, I – I shall dispose of the body.

MILES. Ghoul! I will not leave without the comfort of a proper funeral service!

HYSTERIUM *shakes his head no.* PSEUDOLUS *blocks* MILES*'s view.*

PSEUDOLUS. Sir, do you have time for that? I mean, isn't there a war somewhere you should be – ?

MILES. Silence! I insist on conducting a funeral.

PSEUDOLUS. Yes, sir.

MILES. We need mourners.

PSEUDOLUS. We have them. (*To* SOLDIERS.) Hold him firmly.

SOLDIERS *hold* MILES. PSEUDOLUS *exits into* SENEX*'s house.*

MILES. The poor girl. To have died so young, without ever having experienced . . . me.

PSEUDOLUS *re-enters.*

PSEUDOLUS. Sir, they will be here presently. While we wait, would you like something to eat?

MILES. No, thank you. (*Wails, then blubbers.*) Oh, her bridal bower becomes a burial bier of bitter bereavement.

PSEUDOLUS. Very good. Can you say, 'Titus, the tailor, told ten tall tales to Titania, the titmouse?'

MILES. Do not try to cheer me. I am inconsolable!

COURTESANS *enter from* SENEX*'s house, with a bit of black on their near-nakedness.*

PSEUDOLUS. Gather around, handmaidens of sorrow.

MILES (*sings*).
Sound the flute,
Blow the horn,
Pluck the lute,
Forward . . . mourn!

SOLDIERS *and* COURTESANS *wail so effectively that even* HYSTERIUM *is affected.*

PSEUDOLUS (*tragically, over the body*).
All Crete was at her feet,
All Thrace was in her thrall.
All Sparta loved her sweetness and Gaul . . .
And Spain . . .

MILES.
And Greece . . .

PSEUDOLUS.
And Egypt . . .

MILES.
And Syria . . .

PSEUDOLUS.
And Mesopotamia . . .

MOURNERS.
All Crete was at her feet,
All Thrace was in her thrall.
Oh, why should such a blossom fall?

COURTESANS *pound on bench, frightening* HYSTERIUM, *who falls to the floor. He scrambles back on bench, lies there, his arms unfolded.*

MILES.
Speak the spells,
Chant the charms,
Toll the bells –

PSEUDOLUS (*to* HYSTERIUM).
Fold the arms!

HYSTERIUM *slowly folds his arms.*

Sir, on behalf of the body, I want to thank you for a lovely funeral. I don't know about you, but I've suffered enough. If you will just give me the contract, I shall take the body and . . .

MILES (*paying him no attention*).
Strew the soil,
Strum the lyre,
Spread the oil,
Build the pyre!

PSEUDOLUS. A pyre? What kind of pyre?

MILES. A pyre of fire!

PSEUDOLUS. Oh, a fire pyre!

MILES. She must be burned!

PSEUDOLUS. Burned? Sir . . .

MILES. I want her ashes!

PSEUDOLUS. Captain, I implore you. It is not for us to destroy such loveliness. The Gods are awaiting her. They would not be happy if we sent up a charred virgin!

MILES. I cannot afford to offend the Gods.

PSEUDOLUS. Who can?

MILES (*sings*).
All Crete was at her feet,
But I shall weep no more.
I'll find my consolation as before
Among the simple pleasures of war!

(*Speaks.*) Bring me the contract.

SOLDIER *hands him contract.*

I give her to the Gods.

(*Puts contract on* HYSTERIUM.) Take her then and lay her to rest. And I shall go my melancholy way. Men. (*Starts to go, stops.*) Wait. A farewell kiss.

PSEUDOLUS. Of course. (*Kisses* MILES *on the cheek.*)

MILES. Not you! (*Pushes him aside, bends over* HYSTERIUM.)

PSEUDOLUS. Sir! You mustn't!

MILES. Why not?

PSEUDOLUS. It could make you very sick. The truth is, she died of an illness contracted on Crete.

MILES. What illness?

PSEUDOLUS. The plague!

There is general pandemonium. COURTESANS *scream 'The plague, the plague!' and run about wildly, exiting in all directions.*

MILES. Silence!

PSEUDOLUS. The plague! The plague! Run for your lives! (*To audience.*) Don't just sit there! Run!

MILES *grabs* PSEUDOLUS.

MILES. There is no plague!

PSEUDOLUS. What?

MILES. I have returned this day from Crete, and there is no plague.

PSEUDOLUS. Then what was everyone yelling about?

LYCUS *enters, hides behind pillar.*

MILES (*leans over* HYSTERIUM). This girl is alive!

HYSTERIUM (*jumps up*). And she's going to stay that way! (*Runs off.*)

MILES. Stop! After her, men!

SOLDIERS *run off.*

PSEUDOLUS. I'll get her! (*Runs off in opposite direction.*)

MILES. Wait! (*Chases* PSEUDOLUS.)

LYCUS. Now *all* the courtesans have escaped. Eunuchs! I stand to lose a fortune in flesh!

EUNUCH *enters from* LYCUS*'s house.*

Find the girls! Bring them back!

EUNUCH *exits, chattering.* LYCUS *exits.* HYSTERIUM *re-enters, hiding face with leafy branch.*

HYSTERIUM. I've got to get out of these clothes! I'm calm, I'm calm.

SENEX enters from ERRONIUS's house, spots HYSTERIUM, goes to him.

SENEX. Ah, there you are, my little dove! (*Cooing.*) You don't have to be afraid of me.

Leads HYSTERIUM to bench, seats him on his lap.

My slave has prepared a little feast. I want you to serve it to me in there.

Points to ERRONIUS's house.

Do you understand? Go, then.

HYSTERIUM *exits into* SENEX's *house.* SENEX *exits into* ERRONIUS's *house, singing 'Everybody Ought to Have a Maid.'* HYSTERIUM *pokes his head out of door and ducks back into house as he sees* EUNUCH *enter with* VIBRATA. EUNUCH *pushes her into* LYCUS's *house, exits, chattering.* HYSTERIUM *starts out of house once more as* PSEUDOLUS *runs on, kicks him from behind.*

HYSTERIUM. Pseudolus!

PSEUDOLUS. I ought to give you worse than that! What did you do with the contract?

HYSTERIUM. I gave it to a soldier. He wants to meet me later tonight.

PSEUDOLUS. Well, get it. I need it.

MILES (*offstage*). He dies!

PSEUDOLUS. Look out!

PSEUDOLUS *and* HYSTERIUM *run off in opposite directions.* MILES *runs on, runs off after* HYSTERIUM, *shouting.*

MILES. This way, men! I have found her!

SOLDIER *enters and runs off.* DOMINA *enters, disguised as virgin, removes veil from her face, addresses audience.*

DOMINA. If it's a pretty face he wants . . .

PSEUDOLUS enters behind her, gives her a swift kick. She screams. He exits, LYCUS *enters.*

How dare you! (*She slaps* LYCUS.)

SOLDIER (*offstage*). Here she is! Men, the virgin!

SOLDIER runs on, chases DOMINA *and* LYCUS *off.* EUNUCH *enters with* PANACEA *and* TINTINABULA, *pushes them into* LYCUS's *house. He exits, chattering.* MILES *enters, as* DOMINA *re-enters.*

MILES. My virgin!

DOMINA. Sir, I am not anybody's virgin!

MILES. You made that more than clear when last we met!

He runs off. HYSTERIUM *runs on, behind* DOMINA.

HYSTERIUM. The cause of it all!

Kicks DOMINA in the rear, she screams, he hides behind pillar, as LYCUS runs on.

DOMINA. You, again!

Swings at LYCUS, misses, chases him off. HYSTERIUM runs to LYCUS's house.

HYSTERIUM. I have to get out of these clothes!

SENEX enters from ERRONIUS's house.

SENEX. No, no, my dear. Wrong house.

Chases HYSTERIUM around his house.

HYSTERIUM (*as he comes around the first time*). Leave me alone!

SENEX (*following him on the run*). Ah, you're beautiful when you're angry!

HERO appears on balcony of SENEX's house.

HERO (*calls*). Philia! Philia!

Exits into house. HYSTERIUM *re-appears from behind* SENEX's *house.*

HYSTERIUM. Second time around!

Exits into SENEX's house. PSEUDOLUS runs on, chased by SOLDIERS. PSEUDOLUS leads them among the

*pillars, swings doors open, knocks two of them out and into
the wings, trips* THIRD SOLDIER *who falls.* PSEUDOLUS
runs to him, takes contract from his belt. HERO *appears on
balcony.*

HERO. All is lost?

PSEUDOLUS. All is won! The contract! – This is what you
must do –

HERO *exits into house, as* MILES *runs on, sword drawn.*
PSEUDOLUS *cowers.*

MILES. You die!

LYCUS *runs on.*

The leper!

LYCUS. Unclean! Unclean!

MILES *and* PSEUDOLUS *run off in opposite directions.*
LYCUS *runs off.* SENEX *appears on roof of his house,
coos.*

SENEX. I know you're up here somewhere, my dear. Philia!
Philia!

He disappears from roof as PHILIA *enters from behind*
SENEX'*s house.*

PHILIA. I thought I heard someone call my name.

Exits into SENEX'*s house. Two* EUNUCHS *enter carrying*
GEMINAE. *All exit into* LYCUS'*s house.* DOMINA *enters,
hides behind pillar as* PSEUDOLUS, *disguised as*
EUNUCH, *enters, chattering, leading* GYMNASIA, *exits
with her into* LYCUS'*s house.*

DOMINA. That is where my husband is! (*Knocks on* LYCUS'*s
door.*) I know what goes on in there!

PSEUDOLUS *appears in upper window of* LYCUS'*s house.*

PSEUDOLUS. Who doesn't?

DOMINA *goes to* SENEX'*s house, cautiously looks
around. Unseen by her,* HYSTERIUM *enters from same
house, looks around, then* PHILIA *also enters from house,
looking about. They just miss seeing each other as they go
in and out of house. Suddenly they see one another, scream*

and run behind SENEX's *house.* PSEUDOLUS *enters from* LYCUS's *house, runs to* SENEX's *house, opens door. As* PHILIA *runs on from behind house, he pushes her through the doorway. As* HYSTERIUM *passes,* PSEUDOLUS *kicks him and* HYSTERIUM *tumbles into* ERRONIUS's *house.* DOMINA *chases after* HYSTERIUM. *She is followed by* SENEX *who catches her at* ERRONIUS's *door, pushes her in.*

SENEX (*triumphantly*). At last!

HERO *re-appears on balcony.*

PSEUDOLUS. Hero! The contract! (*Throws contract to him.*) To the harbour!

HERO. What will happen to you?

PSEUDOLUS. Nothing. Here is what I will do. I shall cause a diversion. Then I shall drink a potion which will make me appear as if dead.

HERO *exits into house.* SOLDIER *staggers to his feet.*

SOLDIER. You are under arrest!

PSEUDOLUS *blows at him,* SOLDIER *falls back down.* DOMINA *enters from* ERRONIUS's *house, followed by* SENEX. PSEUDOLUS *ducks into* SENEX's *house.*

DOMINA. Dearest Senex, you saw through my disguise!

SENEX. Yes, beloved.

She embraces him. He looks around for PHILIA.

DOMINA. Forgive me for mistrusting you. My darling, it's just that you have been a little distant these last twenty-nine years.

SENEX (*backing off*). Yes, beloved, yes.

Exits, as she follows.

DOMINA. Senex! Senex!

ERRONIUS (*entering*). Third time around!

Starts for his house, as HYSTERIUM *is entering from same house. Seeing* ERRONIUS, *he runs back in.*

The spirit!

Sneaks over to side of his house. HYSTERIUM *peeks out of door, then tip-toes out, not seeing* ERRONIUS.

Who are you?!

HYSTERIUM *trips and falls.* ERRONIUS *helps him up.*

Let me help you.

HYSTERIUM. Thank you. I am quite all right.

ERRONIUS (*seeing ring*). Wait!

HYSTERIUM. What is it?

ERRONIUS. My dear one! My sweet one! My little one! (*Kisses* HYSTERIUM.)

HYSTERIUM. Why do older men find me so attractive?

ERRONIUS. My daughter!

HYSTERIUM. What?

ERRONIUS. You wear the ring with the gaggle of geese!

HYSTERIUM. I am not your daughter!

MILES *and* SOLDIERS *run on, spot* HYSTERIUM.

MILES. There she is!

ERRONIUS. Yes!

MILES. My virgin!

HYSTERIUM. I am not a virgin!

ERRONIUS. Those filthy pirates!

HYSTERIUM. I am not your daughter! I . . . uh . . . I am an Etruscan dancer.

Dances a few steps as SENEX *re-enters.*

SENEX. Dancing with impatience, my dear?

MILES. Who is it speaks so boldly to my virgin?

SENEX. Your what? She is my maid!

ERRONIUS. She is my daughter!

All tug at HYSTERIUM.

HYSTERIUM. Please! No fighting! That hurts! Please!

In the tussle, without knowing it, HYSTERIUM *loses his wig.*

MILES. You are not the virgin!

HYSTERIUM (*walks into* ERRONIUS'*s arms*). Of course not! I am this old man's baby daughter.

SENEX. Hysterium!

MILES. The eunuch!

ERRONIUS. My daughter is a eunuch?

MILES. Seize that man!

Points to HYSTERIUM. SOLDIERS *point swords at him.*

DOMINA (*entering*). Senex!

MILES. You, again?

SENEX. Sir, you are speaking to my wife!

MILES. You are married to that . . . that . . .

SENEX. Yes, I am married to that . . . that! And I shall thank you to release my slave and remove yourself from in front of my house!

MILES. Your house? This is the house of Lycus.

DOMINA. Lycus?

All babble at once.

MILES. Quiet! I declare this area under martial law!

PSEUDOLUS (*entering from* SENEX'*s house, indicating* HYSTERIUM). Release that man!

MILES. Release that man! (*Recognises* PSEUDOLUS.) You!

PSEUDOLUS. Sir, this quivering creature is blameless. It is I, and I alone, who have caused you this grief.

MILES. Men, unseize him and seize him!

SOLDIERS *surround* PSEUDOLUS.

And now, death by evisceration!

PSEUDOLUS *reacts horribly.*

HYSTERIUM. Oh, Pseudolus!

PSEUDOLUS. Calm, my friend. (*To* MILES.) Sir, I believe a doomed man is allowed a final request?

MILES. Yes.

PSEUDOLUS. Allow me to take my own life.

MILES. Sir, I have seen kings with less courage.

PSEUDOLUS. So have I. Hysterium, the potion. You know the one I mean.

HYSTERIUM. The potion? (*Picks up cup from where he placed it earlier.*)

PSEUDOLUS. Thank you, dear friend. Give the hemlock to Socrates.

HYSTERIUM (*to* SOLDIERS). Which one of you is Socrates?

PSEUDOLUS. Give me that! (*Takes cup, raises it.*) I go to sail on uncharted seas. To the harbour, to the harbour . . .

   PHILIA *and* HERO *sneak out of* SENEX's *house, exit unseen.*

   . . . from which no mariner returns. Farewell.

   Drains potion, dies noisily and elaborately. MILES *leans over him.*

   Kiss me!

   He apparently has taken the wrong potion. Jumps up.

   Somebody kiss me! Anybody! (*To* HYSTERIUM.) I could kill you . . . you darling!

MILES. Seize him!

   SOLDIER *grabs* PSEUDOLUS.

PSEUDOLUS. Thank you! I needed that!

MILES. Stop that!

   Smacks PSEUDOLUS *in back of head.* LYCUS *enters with* PHILIA. HERO *follows.*

LYCUS. Great Miles Gloriosus! I would not reveal my true identity until I could deliver that which I had promised. Sir, I am Lycus. Philia, go to the man who bought you.

   PHILIA *sighs, goes to* SENEX. DOMINA *reacts.*

SENEX. No, no.

PHILIA. Aren't you the . . . ?

SENEX (*whispers*). Quiet! We're under martial law.

LYCUS. *There* is the captain! Captain, here is your virgin.

MILES. And worth the waiting for. (*To* PSEUDOLUS.) Out of the great joy of the occasion, forgiveness. You are free.

PSEUDOLUS. Free . . . to be a slave. (*Slumps against pillar.*)

ERRONIUS. I cannot understand it. There was the ring. The ring with the gaggle of geese.

MILES. What did you say, old man? (MILES *extends his hand.*)

ERRONIUS. The ring!

MILES. Father!

ERRONIUS. You've grown!

They embrace.

PHILIA (*showing ring on chain about her neck*). Are these many geese a gaggle?

ERRONIUS. How long have you had this?

PHILIA. I've had this since, I don't know when I've had this since.

ERRONIUS. My daughter!

MILES. My sister?!

HYSTERIUM. Pseudolus, did you hear that?

PSEUDOLUS. Silence! Stand back, everyone! My dear old man, I take it your daughter is free born?

ERRONIUS. Without a doubt!

PSEUDOLUS. Lycus, as all of us know, the penalty for selling a free-born citizen is to be trampled to death by a water buffalo in heat!

MILES. Seize him!

LYCUS. Careful, I'm a bleeder!

PSEUDOLUS (*to* LYCUS). Bring out those girls! (*To audience.*)
I told you this was to be a comedy!

As LYCUS *brings* COURTESANS *out of his house.*

Hero!

HERO. Mother and father, I wish to marry.

SENEX (*aside*). Son, if you are only as happy as your mother
and I, my heart will bleed for you.

PSEUDOLUS
(*sings, to audience, indicating* HERO *and* PHILIA).
Lovers divided
Get coincided.
Something for everyone –

HERO *and* PHILIA.
A comedy tonight!

PSEUDOLUS (*indicating* SENEX *and* DOMINA).
Father and mother
Get one another.

DOMINA.
Something for everyone –

SENEX.
A tragedy tonight!

MILES (*holding the* GEMINAE).
I get the twins!
They get the best!

ERRONIUS.
I get a family . . .

HYSTERIUM.
I get a rest.

SOLDIERS (*holding the other* COURTESANS).
We get a few girls.

LYCUS.
I'll get some new girls.

PSEUDOLUS.
I get the thing I want to be:
Free!

ALL.
> Free! Free! Free! Free! Free!

PSEUDOLUS *exits joyfully.*

> Nothing for kings,
> Nothing for crowns,
> Something for lovers, liars and clowns!
> What is the moral?
> Must be a moral.
> Here is the moral, wrong or right:

PSEUDOLUS (*re-entering with* GYMNASIA).
> Morals tomorrow!

ALL.
> Comedy, comedy, comedy, comedy, comedy, comedy,
> Comedy, comedy,
> Tonight!

Curtain.

ADDITIONAL LYRICS
with commentary by Stephen Sondheim

'Invocation' and 'Love Is in the Air'

'Invocation' was the original opening number for the show, but the director, George Abbott, felt that the tune wasn't hummable enough, so I replaced it with 'Love Is in the Air', which we used during the try-out in New Haven and Washington. The problem with 'Love Is in the Air' was that it misled the audience into believing that they were going to see a charming vaudeville instead of a knockabout farce. When Jerome Robbins came to Washington to help us out, he suggested to me that the opening number should be a bouncy song with a neutral lyric so that he could stage a collage of low-comedy vignettes against it. The result was 'Comedy Tonight', which was staged with brilliant invention and which overnight turned the show from a flop into a hit.

'Invocation'

COMPANY *(to the Gods).*
    Gods of the theatre, smile on us.
    You who sit up there stern in judgment, smile on us.
    You who look down on actors (and who doesn't?),
    Bless our little company and smile on us.
    Think not about deep concerns,
    Think not about dark dilemmas.
    We offer you rites and revels,
    Smile on us for a while.

To the audience.

    Gods of the theatre, smile on us.
    You who sit out there stern in judgment, smile on us.
    Think not about deep concerns,
    Think not about dark dilemmas.

We offer you rites and revels,
Bless our play and smile.

Forget war, forget woe,
Forget matters weighty and great,
Allow matters weighty to wait
For a while.
For this moment, this brief time,
Frown on reason, smile on rhyme.

Forget pomp, forget show,
Forget laurels, helmets and crowns,
Receive lovers, liars and clowns
For a while.
For this brief moment, this brief span,
Celebrate the state of man.

Forget war, forget woe,
Forget greed and vengeance and sin
And let mime and mockery in
For a while.

Gods of the theatre, smile on us.
Gods of the theatre, bless our efforts, smile on us.
We offer you song and dance,
We offer you rites and revels,
Grace and beauty,
Joy and laughter,
Sly disguises,
Wild confusions,
Happy endings.
If we please you,
Bless our play,
Smile our way.
Smile this moment, then at length
Go, and with a new-found strength

Resume war, resume woe,
Resume matters weighty and great,
Resume man's impossible state,
But now smile.
For this moment,
This brief stay,
Bless these players,
Bless this play!

'Love Is in the Air'

PROLOGUS *and* PROTEANS.

> Love is in the air
> Quite clearly.
> People everywhere
> Act queerly.
> Some are hasty, some are halting,
> Some are simply somersaulting,
> Love is going around.
>
> Anyone exposed
> Can catch it.
> Keep your window closed
> And latch it.
> Leave your house and lose your reason,
> This is the contagious season:
> Love is going around.
>
> It's spreading each minute
> Throughout the whole vicinity,
> Step out and you're in it:
> With all the fun involved,
> Who can stay uninvolved?
>
> Love is in the air
> This morning.
> Bachelors beware,
> Fair warning:
> If you start to feel a tingle
> And you like remaining single,
> Stay home, don't take a breath,
> You could catch your death,
> 'Cause love is around.

'Farewell'

This song was written specifically for Nancy Walker when she agreed to play Domina in the 1971 revival.

Cue into 'Farewell':

DOMINA. Senex, lead the way!

SENEX. Yes, dear.

DOMINA. Oversee the slaves.

SENEX. Yes, dear.

DOMINA. And Senex –

SENEX. Yes, dear?

DOMINA. Carry my bust with pride.

SENEX *(to audience)*. A lesson for you all. Never fall in love during a total eclipse! *(Exits.)*

DOMINA *(sings).*
Farewell, beloved son.

Kisses HERO.

Farewell, devoted slave.

HYSTERIUM *kisses her hem.*

Farewell, my ancestral home.
Farewell, my Rome.

Farewell, you temples and basilicae,
More rich than Athens or Pompeii.
Though country life be more idyllic, I
Could never long stay away.

Farewell, responsive son.

Kisses HERO.

Farewell, respectful slave.

HYSTERIUM *kisses her hand.*

Farewell, resplendent Rome.
Farewell, my home.
Farewell.

Exits. HYSTERIUM *starts to rise and* HERO *opens his mouth to talk to him when suddenly* DOMINA *re-enters;* HYSTERIUM *immediately falls to his knees again.* DOMINA *caresses her house.*

Farewell, inestimable domicile.
Farewell, domestic work of art.
Although I journey far, I promise I'll

Keep every portico,
Every pediment,
Every plinth in my heart –
I start.

Farewell, angelic son.
Farewell, efficient slave.
Farewell, exquisite Rome.
Farewell, my home.
Farewell!

Exits. Again, HYSTERIUM *and* HERO *start to continue the action, but again* DOMINA *re-enters.*

Could anyone conceive a view
More beautiful than this and these?
One look before I take my leave of you:

Sentimentally, to HYSTERIUM.

So scrub my atrium, leave it stainless.
Wash my architrave when it's rainless.
Keep my progeny chaste and brainless . . .
Please,
No tears . . .

Standing back from them.

My frieze . . .
My dears . . .
Farewell, beloved son.

Kisses HERO.

Farewell, devoted slave.

Is kissed by HYSTERIUM.

Farewell, ancestral home.
Farewell, my Rome, farewell.
Farewell.

Exiting, her voice fading into the distance.

Farewell . . . farewell . . . farewell . . . etc. . . .

HYSTERIUM *and* HERO *wait until her voice has faded almost into nothingness, then start once more to resume the action only to have* DOMINA *re-enter again, this time from the other side of the stage.*

Farewell!

She exits for good.

The action continues with HYSTERIUM's *speech, 'Well, to work, to work!'*

'The House of Marcus Lycus'

This was cut down to a minimum because Burt felt strongly that the presentation of the girls from the House of Lycus should be either a dance or a song, but not both – and since there was so much singing in the expository first forty-five minutes of the show, we opted for the dance.

LYCUS *(as* FEMINA *enters and parades).* To make her available to you, I outbid the King of Nubia. Femina. With a face that holds a thousand promises . . . and a body that stands behind each promise.

Sings.

Hot-blooded, cool-headed, warm-hearted, sly.
Light-footed, dark-featured, dim-witted, shy.
Only recently arrived from Greece,
Likes her love experimental.
Every inch of her a masterpiece –
High standards, low rental . . .

As VIBRATA *enters, speaks.*

Now may I present Vibrata. Exotic as a jungle bloom, wondrous as a flamingo, lithe as a panther . . . For the man whose interest is – wild life.

Sings.

Uncanny, unnerving, unblemished, untaught,
Unstinting, unswerving, unselfish, unbought.
Here's potential that is still untapped,
Here are fires still unstarted.
Here are raptures that are still unwrapped,
Whole sections uncharted . . .

PSEUDOLUS.

Hot-blooded, warm-hearted . . .

LYCUS

Unselfish, uncharted . . .

There is merchandise for
every mood

Light-footed, dark-featured . . .

At the House of Marcus
Lycus.

Unblemished, dim-witted . . .

There is latitude and
longitude

Cool-headed, low rental . . .

At the House of Marcus
Lycus.

Unstinting, unswerving . . .

'Neath the cherry-blossom
and the quince
And the cooing of the dove,
At the House of Marcus Lycus,
Prince of Love.

Speaks, as a very tall girl enters.

And now – Gymnasia! A stadium of delight. A province of
mystery. A challenge to the intrepid explorer.

Sings.

Expansive, explosive, exquisite and excruciating,
Exceeding exciting, exhausting but exhilarating . . .
Wait until the day she's fully grown –
She'll be useful on safari.
You could purchase her for shade alone
And never be sorry.

Speaks.

What's that you say? 'Hold! Enough! I am dazzled!' And to
that I say, but wait . . .

As twins enter.

May I present the Geminae. A matched pair. Either one a
divinely assembled woman, together an infinite number of
mathematical possibilities.

Sings.

A banquet, a bargain, placed end to end.
A lifetime's provisions – invite a friend.
Feast until you're fully satisfied,

Gorge on gorgeousness compounded.
Face the future side by side by side,
Completely surrounded . . .

PSEUDOLUS.

LYCUS.   Completely . . .

No taxes . . .

A lifetime's . . .

Don't handle . . .   GIRLS.

Unblemished . . .   You can feast until
                                            you're satisfied

One birthmark . . . A banquet . . .   At the House of
                                            Marcus Lycus.

A bargain . . .   Exhausting . . .   Face the future side
                                            by side by side

Don't *do* that!   A lifetime's . . . At the House of
                                            Marcus Lycus.

For a sense of
                                            sensuality

And a plethora
                                            thereof . . .

LYCUS.

One is ecstasy,
One is mystery,
One is six foot three,
Two is company –
At the House of Marcus Lycus,
Merchant of Love!

Speaks.

And need I add, as all who are of the House of Lycus, these
beauties are well-versed in the arts, proficient at needlework
and surprised at nothing.

'Your Eyes Are Blue'

*This song was written for Hero and Philia when they first meet
in Act One. We used it during the New Haven try-out, but cut it
when our two young leading players, Pat Fox and Karen Black,
were replaced by Brian Davies and Preshy Marker.*

HERO.
> Once upon a time
> It happened there lived a boy
> Who loved a girl . . .
> Your eyes are blue . . .
> And every single night
> He'd see her across the way.
> I'd want to say –
> *He'd* want to say,
> 'Your eyes are blue
> And I love you.'

> But never had they spoken,
> Never had he dared.
> Beautiful as she was,
> I was –
> *He* was
> Scared.

> Then suddenly one day
> He met her, and he could see
> Her eyes were blue
> As they could be.
> What did he do?
> Well . . .
> You tell me.

> Once upon a time –

PHILIA.
> Let me try –
> 'There lived a boy . . . '

HERO.
> 'Who loved a girl . . . '

PHILIA.
> 'Whose eyes were –
> Blue!'
> And every single night
> She'd see him across the way.
> She hoped he'd say,
> 'Your eyes are blue
> And I love you!'
> And yet she knew . . .

    There was a wall between them
    Built around his heart.
    This was their dilemma,
    Keeping them apart,
    When suddenly one day
    She met him . . .
    He looked so tall . . .

HERO.
    He felt so small . . .

PHILIA.
    What did he do

    To break the wall?

HERO.
    What could he do
    To break the wall?

They kiss.

BOTH.
    And that was
    All.

'I Do Like You'

This number was to be sung by Hysterium and Pseudolus in Act One just before Hysterium goes off to the country to snitch on Pseudolus. It never got beyond the early stages of rehearsals for reasons too dimly buried for me to remember. It was replaced by Pseudolus's 'erotic pottery' speech.

PSEUDOLUS.
    Friend,

    Good
    Friend and true,

    I worship
    You.

    I
    Want to do,
    Want to be

HYSTERIUM.
    Oh, today it's
    'Friend' . . .
    Yes,
    It's always
    'Friend' . . .

    When you need a
    Friend.

Like my
Friend.   'Friend, friend, friend, friend,
Do   Friend' . . .
What you must.   That's
                                 What I in-
I'm   Tend . . .
Happy just   Well, goodbye, old
Being   Friend . . .
A copy of the one I
Trust.

PSEUDOLUS.

I like to do like you like to do,
'Cause I like you . . .

HYSTERIUM.

Oh, Pseudolus!

PSEUDOLUS.

You do a deed,
I follow your lead,
'Cause I like you.

HYSTERIUM.

Oh, Pseudolus!

PSEUDOLUS.

You climb a tree,
I climb with you.
You give a smile,
I smile.
You take a journey,
I'm with you!
Whatever you'll do,
I'll.

No one is perfect,
You have your flaws,
But I don't care.
I have the flaws
That you have because
I want to share.
You're all the things
I most admire,
All I aspire
To.

I do like you
Because I do like you.

HYSTERIUM.

PSEUDOLUS
    Friend,

  And the best you
  Have . . .
    You've touched me
  Yes,
    So.
  I thought I
  Would . . .
    I didn't
  No, you never
    Know
  Do . . .
    Such deep devotion
    Existed and

  Deeper than you
    Friend,
  Think . . .
    I'd rather
  You don't have to
    Die
  Die . . .
    Than say good-
  I know how you
    Bye.
  Feel . . .
    Friend, just as
    Soon as I get back I'll cry.

PSEUDOLUS.

  I like to do like you like to do,
  That's how I feel.
  You ruin me, and I ruin you,
  You're my ideal.
  We each have had a fling
  Or two,
  Nobody knows but we.
  You tell a little thing
  Or two,
  I tell a thing or three.

  You keep a secret, I keep a secret
  Like I should.
  You tell a secret, I tell a secret
  Twice as good.
  Since you're the model I take after
  That's what I'd have to do.
  I have to do like you like,
  Only because I do like
  You.

PSEUDOLUS *and* HYSTERIUM.
> Reciprocation in the end
> Is why a friend
> Is true.
> How could I ever doubt you?
> Knowing so much about you.
> I do like you
> And still I do like you.

'There's Something About a War'

This never even got into rehearsal. Burt felt that there should be no political or satirical edge to any of the songs, since the show was to be strictly a domestic farce and not a commentary. It was replaced by 'Bring Me My Bride' (which, incidentally, used the only line in the show directly translated from Plautus: 'I am a parade').

MILES *(entering, with the* PROTEANS *dressed as* SOLDIERS).
> Stand aside there, I take large steps!

SOLDIERS.
> One-two, one-two!

MILES.
> We not only fought but we won, too!

SOLDIERS.
> One-two, one-two!
> Left-right, left-right!

MILES.
> There's none of the enemy left, right?

SOLDIERS *(confused)*.
> Right! Left-right, left-Left-uh-right!

MILES.
> Halt!

> *Front.*

> I don't know how to say it,
> But there's something about a war.
> Mere words cannot convey it, ·

But there's something about a war.
It's noisy and it's crowded and you have to stand in line,
But there's something about a war
That's divine!

You march until you're bleary,
But there's something about a war.
The company is dreary,
But there's something about a war.
Your fingernails get broken and the food is often vile,
But there's something about a war
Makes you smile.

The rain may rust your armour,
Your straps may be too tight,
But decapitate a farmer
And your heart feels light!

There's something about a war,
Something about a war,
Something about a war
That makes this little old world all right.

MILES *and* SOLDIERS *(variously)*.
Oh, it's tread, tread, tread
Through the mud, mud, mud
And it's shed, shed, shed
All the blood, blood – yich!

MILES, *then* SOLDIERS.
There's something about a war.

MILES *and* SOLDIERS *(variously)*.
Oh, it's plunge, plunge, plunge
Through the dust, dust, dust
And it's lunge, lunge, lunge
And it's thrust, thrust – oooh!

MILES, *then* SOLDIERS.
There's something about a war.

ALL.
You know it isn't massacres and laughter all day long,
Still there's something about a war –

A SOLDIER.
Like a song!

MILES.

A warrior's work is never done,
He never can take a rest.
There always are lands to overrun
And people to be oppressed.

SOLDIERS (*variously*).

There's always a town to pillage,
A city to be laid to waste.
There's always a little village
Entirely to be erased.
And citadels to sack, of course,
And temples to attack, of course,
Children to annihilate,
Priestesses to violate,
Houses to destroy – hey!
Women to enjoy – hey!
Statues to deface – hey!
Mothers to debase – hey!
Virgins to assault – hey!

MILES.

Halt – hey!

Front.

It's hurry, hurry, hurry,
But there's something about a war.
It's worry after worry,
But there's something about a war.
It isn't all the drama and heroics it may seem –

ALL.

But there's something about a war
That's a scream!

MILES.

There's never time for reading,
Yet there's something about a war.
The elephants keep breeding,
But there's something about a war.
You frequently feel lonely when the enemy has gone,
Still there's something about a war
That goes on!

ALL.
>And on! And on!

MILES.
>You sulk when someone's suing
>For temporary truce,
>Then another war starts brewing
>And soon breaks loose!

ALL.
>There's something about a war,

MILES, *then* SOLDIERS.
>Something about a war –

MILES.
>It isn't just the glory or
>The groaning or the gorier
>Details that cause a warrior
>To smirk.

SOLDIERS.
>Left-right!

ALL.
>It's the knowledge that he'll never be out of work!

'Echo Song'

'Echo Song' was cut in New Haven during the try-out because the whole show wasn't working properly and this number (among many others) didn't make enough impact on the audience. It was replaced by 'That'll Show Him', which was transferred from Act One to Act Two. Burt Shevelove and I decided to resuscitate 'Echo Song' for the 1971 revival, where once again it didn't work. It did seem, however, to be more effective than 'That'll Show Him' if for no other reason than that it offered some funny staging opportunities.

Cue into 'Echo Song' (replacing the one into 'That'll Show Him'):

HERO. I hate him.

PHILIA. So do I.

HERO. What shall we do?

PHILIA. If you ask the Gods for guidance, they sometimes answer you by echoing your words.

HERO. Echoing your words?

PHILIA. Instead of those other things. Like thunder.

Music under.

HERO *(looking at the roof, getting an idea)*. Perhaps if you were alone the Gods would listen more closely.

PHILIA. Perhaps. I shall pray.

As she starts to sing, facing front, HERO *clambers to the roof to answer her hollowly as a god.*

Tell me . . .
Dare I ask it? . . .
Should I love him? . . .
Shall I leave with him? . . .
Tell me . . .
Should I leave right now? . . .
I hear my heart say,
'Let him live with me!'
Should I hear my heart and go?

Turns away discouraged, tries again.

Tell me . . .

           HERO *(sings)*.
           (Tell me . . .)

Dare I ask it? . . .

           (Ask it.)

Should I love him? . . .

           (Love him!)

Shall I leave with him? . . .

           (Leave with him, leave with him!)

Tell me . . .

           (Tell me . . .)

Should I leave right now? . . .

           (Right now!)

I hear my heart say,
'Let him live with me!'

           (Live with me, live with me!)

Should I hear my heart and go?

> (Go! Go!)

Or should I, worthy, wait here
Till I meet my fate here?
Tell me, tell me, I must know.

> (No, no, no . . .)

Tell me . . .

> (Tell me . . .)

Should I hold him? . . .

> (Hold him!)

Or forget him

> (Get him!)

And forego my love?

> (Go, my love! Go, my love!)

Thank you!

> (Thank you!)

I believe, now!

> (Leave now!)

I must hurry,

> (Hurry!)

So I'll say goodbye.

> (Say goodbye, say goodbye!)

Only one more question,
   please –

> (Please! Please! Please!)

Does he want me?

> (Does he!)

Would he miss me?

> (Would he!)

Must I pay the debt I owe?

> (Oh . . . Oh . . .)

Or may I go with Hero,
My beloved Hero?
Tell me yes, so I may know.

> (Ye – N – Y – N – Yes!)

At the end of the song, PHILIA *realises that it is* HERO *she has been listening to, and looks up to see him.*

PHILIA. Oh, Hero, you have enraged the Gods!

HERO (*jumping down*). I don't care!

PHILIA. But they will strike you down.

HERO. Oh, let them. I would die for love of you!

PHILIA. You would die for me?

HERO. Die dead.

PHILIA. Oh, Hero, if you could get the contract from the Captain, I would go with you.

HERO. Dare I dare believe what you are saying?

PHILIA. You dare dare.

PSEUDOLUS *enters from* LYCUS*'s house.*

'The Gaggle of Geese'

This song never got into rehearsal. It was cut because the situation that gave rise to it was cut when we were shortening the script. The situation: Pseudolus, for reasons too complicated to explain here, had drunk a knock-out potion and was lying unconscious in front of Erronius's house, wearing the ring with the gaggle of geese. While Hysterium is trying desperately to bring him back to life, Erronius stumbles on, trips over the body, sees the ring and assumes that Pseudolus is his long-lost son, stolen in infancy by pirates.

ERRONIUS (*suddenly emits a series of inarticulate cries, to music*). Eeeeh! Aaaahh!

HYSTERIUM *reacts*; ERRONIUS *staggers.*

Aaahh! Eeeeh!

HYSTERIUM (*ad lib*). What's the matter?

ERRONIUS.
Aahh . . . eeehh . . . aahh . . . eeehh . . . eeehh . . . aahh . . . The ring! The ring!

HYSTERIUM. What ring?

ERRONIUS.
He's wearing the ring!
The ring with the gaggle of geese!

HYSTERIUM. Gaggle of *what?*

ERRONIUS.
>It's proof! You see?
>There only are three!
>They're worn by my children and me!

HYSTERIUM. I don't follow . . .

ERRONIUS.
>The family crest, the gaggle of geese,
>The ring with the galloping gaggle of geese!

>The Gods above
>Have answered my call!
>Release every dove
>From Carthage to Gaul!
>Light welcoming fires, let trumpets and lyres
>Proclaim it to one and to all:
>THIS IS MY SON!

>The gaggle of geese, the gaggle of geese,
>It *is* the gaggle of geese,
>For years I've sought the gaggle of geese,
>And here is the gaggle of geese
>At last, the gaggle of geese!

>The gaggle of geese, the gaggle of geese!
>It's not a covey of quails,
>It's not a flight of nightingales,
>It isn't a school of whales,
>It must be a gaggle of geese!

>Sing paeans of jubilation
>In celebration!
>Send runners with torches burning
>To mark my son's returning!

>The gaggle of geese, the gaggle of geese!
>Ring out . . . the gaggle . . . the bells . . .
>The geese . . . My son . . . the gaggle . . . is home . . .
>Again . . . with the gaggle . . . he wears . . .
>To stay . . . with the gaggle . . .

>My heart has joy,
>My mind has peace,
>I've found my boy

With the gaggle of – look! The gaggle of – see! The gaggle
  of – yes!
The gaggle of – this! The gaggle of – there!

Speaking, music under.

Hysterium, why are you sitting around?
It isn't enough that my son has been found!
My daughter, my daughter, yes, where is my daughter?
And why is my boy lying down on the ground?
Do something at once! He's obviously
Completely exhausted from searching for me.
Go get a physician!
No, stay with him here and *I'll* get a physician –
No, first I will seek that sayer of sooth –
He'll certainly know where my daughter must be!
My son being here, she ought to be near . . .
Not here . . . but where? . . . Nearby, but where? . . .
He'll know . . . I go . . .
Goodbye . . .
Hello,
My beautiful boy!

Covers the prostrate PSEUDOLUS *with kisses; a great
smile spreads over* PSEUDOLUS*'s face.*

The family crest
Was put to the test
And half of my quest
Is done!
I have at long last found my long-lost son!

*He starts offstage, bumps into the sundial, pats it
affectionately.*

Forgive me, my child . . . Go back to your game . . .

Continues off, bumps into proscenium, calls into wings.

Wait for me, daughter, wherever you are! . . .

Exits.